STEPHEN CHBOSKY

THE PERKS OF BEING A WALLFLOWER

Cornelsen

Stephen Chbosky
The Perks of Being a Wallflower

Herausgegeben von:
Gunthild Porteous-Schwier, Ingrid Ross

Verlagsredaktion: Neil Porter

Technische Umsetzung: Peter Richter

Umschlagillustrationen:
Großes Bild: "Wallflower textile" (Victoria & Albert Museum; BILDARCHIV STEFFENS/Bridgeman Art Library)
Kleines Bild: "Teenager Looking over Water" (© Walter Lopez/Corbis)

First published by MTV Books/Pocket Books, a Division of Simon & Schuster Inc.

Herausgeber der *Cornelsen Senior English Library:*
Prof. Dr. Albert-Reiner Glaap

www.cornelsen.de

1. Auflage, 3. Druck 2006

Alle Drucke dieser Auflage sind inhaltlich unverändert und können im Unterricht nebeneinander verwendet werden.

Druck: Druckerei zu Altenburg

ISBN-13: 978-3-464-36000-2
ISBN-10: 3-464-36000-8

Inhalt gedruckt auf säurefreiem Papier aus nachhaltiger Forstwirtschaft.

CONTENTS

For my family

Acknowledgments

I just wanted to say about all those listed that there would be no book without them, and I thank them with all of my heart.

Greer Kessel Hendricks
Heather Neely
Lea, Fred, and Stacy Chbosky
Robbie Thompson
Christopher McQuarrie
Margaret Mehring
Stewart Stern
Kate Degenhart
Mark McClain Wilson
David Wilcox
Kate Ward
Tim Perell
Jack Horner
Eduardo Braniff

And finally …
Dr. Earl Reum for writing a beautiful poem
and Patrick Comeaux for remembering it wrong when he was 14.

Abbreviations

adj	adjective
adv	adverb
AE	American English
BE	British English
cf.	confer; see
derog	derogatory
e.g.	exempli gratia; for example
esp.	especially
etc.	et cetera; and so on
fml	formal
i.e.	id est; in other words
infml	informal
jdm./jdn.	jemandem/en
n	noun
p., pp.	page, pages
pl	plural
sb.	somebody
sl	slang
sth.	something
usu.	usually
v	verb

The annotations are arranged chronologically: the first time a word is used is where you will find it explained. All pronunciations given are American English; where two pronunciations are given, the first is the standard American English, the second (after the letters BE) the standard British English pronunciation. Regular differences between British and American pronunciation have not been given. Regular spelling differences (e.g. *color* versus *colour*) between American and British are not indicated.

part 1

August 25, 1991

Dear friend,

I am writing to you because she said you listen and understand and didn't try to sleep with that person at that party even though you could have. Please don't try to figure out who she is because then you might figure out who I am, and I really don't want you to do that. I will call people by different names or generic names because I don't want you to find me. I didn't enclose a return address for the same reason. I mean nothing bad by this. Honest.

I just need to know that someone out there listens and understands and doesn't try to sleep with people even if they could have. I need to know that these people exist.

I think you of all people would understand that because I think you of all people are alive and appreciate what that means. At least I hope you do because other people look to you for strength and friendship and it's that simple. At least that's what I've heard.

So, this is my life. And I want you to know that I am both happy and sad and I'm still trying to figure out how that could be.

I try to think of my family as a reason for me being this way, especially after my friend Michael stopped going to school one day last spring and we heard Mr. Vaughn's voice on the loudspeaker.

"Boys and girls, I regret to inform you that one of our students has passed on. We will hold a memorial service for Michael Dobson during assembly this Friday."

I don't know how news travels around school and why it is very often right. Maybe it was in the lunchroom. It's hard to remember. But Dave with the awkward glasses told us that Michael killed himself. His mom played bridge with one of Michael's neighbors and they heard the gunshot.

I don't really remember much of what happened after that except that my older brother came to Mr. Vaughn's office in my middle school and told me to stop crying. Then, he put his arm on my shoulder and told me to get it out of my system before Dad came home. We then went to eat french fries at McDonald's and he taught me how to play pinball. He even made a joke that because of me he got to skip an afternoon of school and asked me if I wanted to help him work on his Camaro. I guess I was pretty messy because he never let me work on his Camaro before.

At the guidance counselor sessions, they asked the few of us who actually liked Michael to say a few words. I think they were afraid that some of us would try to kill ourselves or something because they looked very tense and one of them kept touching his beard.

Bridget who is crazy said that sometimes she thought about suicide when commercials come on during TV. She was sincere and this puzzled the guidance counselors. Carl who is nice to everyone said that he felt very sad, but could never kill himself because it is a sin.

This one guidance counselor went through the whole group and finally came to me.

"What do you think, Charlie?"

What was so strange about this was the fact that I had never met this man because he was a "specialist" and he knew my name even though I wasn't wearing a name tag like they do in open house.

"Well, I think that Michael was a nice guy and I don't understand why he did it. As much as I feel sad, I think that not knowing is what really bothers me."

I just reread that and it doesn't sound like how I talk. Especially in that office because I was crying still. I never did stop crying.

The counselor said that he suspected that Michael had "problems at home" and didn't feel like he had anyone to talk to. That's maybe why he felt all alone and killed himself.

Then, I started screaming at the guidance counselor that Michael could have talked to me. And I started crying even harder. He tried to calm me down by saying that he meant an adult like a teacher or a guidance counselor. But it didn't work and eventually my brother came by the middle school in his Camaro to pick me up.

For the rest of the school year, the teachers treated me different and gave me better grades even though I didn't get any smarter. To tell you the truth, I think I made them all nervous.

▷ **5** *figure sth. out:* think about sth. until you understand it **7** *generic:* referring to the type (and not the specific characteristics) of a person or thing **23** *pass on:* die **31–32** *middle school:* (cf. Vocabulary: "Going to School in America"; p. 182) **33** *get sth. out of your system* (infml): deal with sth. (usu. an unpleasant emotion) so that it no longer bothers you **36** *get to do sth.* (AE infml): be allowed to do sth. **37** *Camaro:* type of car • *messy* = *messed up:* in a bad state of mind **39** *guidance counselor:* (cf. p. 182) **53** *open house* (BE: *open day*): (cf. p. 182) **68** *grades:* (cf. p. 181)

Michael's funeral was strange because his father didn't cry. And three months later he left Michael's mom. At least according to Dave at lunchtime. I think about it sometimes. I wonder what went on in Michael's house around dinner and TV shows. Michael never left a note or at least his parents didn't let anyone see it. Maybe it was "problems at home." I wish I knew. It might make me miss him more clearly. It might have made sad sense.

One thing I do know is that it makes me wonder if I have "problems at home" but it seems to me that a lot of other people have it a lot worse. Like when my sister's first boyfriend started going around with another girl and my sister cried for the whole weekend.

My dad said, "There are other people who have it a lot worse."

And my mom was quiet. And that was that. A month later, my sister met another boy and started playing happy records again. And my dad kept working. And my mom kept sweeping. And my brother kept fixing his Camaro. That is, until he left for college at the beginning of the summer. He's playing football for Penn State but he needed the summer to get his grades right to play football.

I don't think that there is a favorite kid in our family. There are three of us and I am the youngest. My brother is the oldest. He is a very good football player and likes his car. My sister is very pretty and mean to boys and she is in the middle. I get straight A's now like my sister and that is why they leave me alone.

My mom cries a lot during TV programs. My dad works a lot and is an honest man. My Aunt Helen used to say that my dad was going to be too proud to have a midlife crisis. It took me until around now to understand what she meant by that because he just turned forty and nothing has changed.

My Aunt Helen was my favorite person in the whole world. She was my mom's sister. She got straight A's when she was a teenager and she used to give me books to read. My father said that the books were a little too old for me, but I liked them so he just shrugged and let me read.

My Aunt Helen lived with the family for the last few years of her life because something very bad happened to her. Nobody would tell me what happened then even though I always wanted to know. When I was around seven, I stopped asking about it because I kept asking like kids always do and my Aunt Helen started crying very hard.

That's when my dad slapped me, saying, "You're hurting your aunt Helen's feelings!" I didn't want to do that, so I stopped. Aunt Helen told my father not to hit me in front of her ever again and my father said this was his house and he would do what he wanted and my mom was quiet and so were my brother and sister.

I don't remember much more than that because I started crying really hard and after a while my dad had my mom take me to my room. It wasn't until much later that my mom had a few glasses of white wine and told me what happened to her sister. Some people really do have it a lot worse than I do. They really do.

I should probably go to sleep now. It's very late. I don't know why I wrote a lot of this down for you to read. The reason I wrote this letter is because I start high school tomorrow and I am really afraid of going.

Love always,
Charlie

September 7, 1991

Dear friend,

I do not like high school. The cafeteria is called the "Nutrition Center," which is strange. There is this one girl in my advanced english class named Susan. In middle school, Susan was very fun to be around. She liked movies, and her brother Frank made her tapes of this great music that she shared with us. But over the summer she had her braces taken off, and she got a little taller and prettier and grew breasts. Now, she acts a lot dumber in the hallways, especially when boys are around. And I think it's sad because Susan doesn't look as happy. To tell you the truth, she doesn't like to admit she's in the advanced english class, and she doesn't like to say "hi" to me in the hall anymore.

When Susan was at the guidance counselor meeting about Michael, she said that Michael once told her that she was the prettiest

▷ **17** *Penn State:* the Pennsylvania State University **22** *straight A's:* (cf. "grades", p. 181) **59** *english* (non-standard): English **62** *braces:* Zahnklammer

girl in the whole world, braces and all. Then, he asked her to "go with him," which was a big deal at any school. They call it "going out" in high school. And they kissed and talked about movies, and she missed him terribly because he was her best friend.

It's funny, too, because boys and girls normally weren't best friends around my school. But Michael and Susan were. Kind of like my Aunt Helen and me. I'm sorry. "My Aunt Helen and I." That's one thing I learned this week. That and more consistent punctuation.

I keep quiet most of the time, and only one kid named Sean really seemed to notice me. He waited for me after gym class and said really immature things like how he was going to give me a "swirlie," which is where someone sticks your head in the toilet and flushes to make your hair swirl around. He seemed pretty unhappy as well, and I told him so. Then, he got mad and started hitting me, and I just did the things my brother taught me to do. My brother is a very good fighter.

"Go for the knees, throat, and eyes."

And I did. And I really hurt Sean. And then I started crying. And my sister had to leave her senior honors class and drive me home. I got called to Mr. Small's office, but I didn't get suspended or anything because a kid told Mr. Small the truth about the fight.

"Sean started it. It was self-defense."

And it was. I just don't understand why Sean wanted to hurt me. I didn't do anything to him. I am very small. That's true. But I guess Sean didn't know I could fight. The truth is I could have hurt him a lot worse. And maybe I should have. I thought I might have to if he came after the kid who told Mr. Small the truth, but Sean never did go after him. So, everything was forgotten.

Some kids look at me strange in the hallways because I don't decorate my locker, and I'm the one who beat up Sean and couldn't stop crying after he did it. I guess I'm pretty emotional.

It has been very lonely because my sister is busy being the oldest one in our family. My brother is busy being a football player at Penn State. After the training camp, his coach said that he was second string and that when he starts learning the system, he will be first string.

My dad really hopes he will make it to the pros and play for the Steelers. My mom is just glad he gets to go to college for free because my sister doesn't play football, and there wouldn't be enough money to send both of them. That's why she wants me to keep working hard, so I'll get an academic scholarship.

So, that's what I'm doing until I meet a friend here. I was hoping that the kid who told the truth could become a friend of mine, but I think he was just being a good guy by telling.

Love always,
Charlie

September 11, 1991

Dear friend,

I don't have a lot of time because my advanced english teacher assigned us a book to read, and I like to read books twice. Incidentally, the book is *To Kill a Mockingbird*. If you haven't read it, I think you should because it is very interesting. The teacher has assigned us a few chapters at a time, but I do not like to read books like that. I am halfway through the first time.

Anyway, the reason I am writing to you is because I saw my brother on television. I normally don't like sports too much, but this was a special occasion. My mother started crying, and my father put his arm around her shoulder, and my sister smiled, which is funny because my brother and sister always fight when he's around.

But my older brother was on television, and so far, it has been the highlight of my two weeks in high school. I miss him terribly, which is strange, because we never really talked much when he was here. We still don't talk, to be honest.

▷ **8** *consistent:* sticking to a system • *punctuation:* Interpunktion **9** *Sean* [ʃɔːn] **18** *senior:* (cf. p. 183) • *honors class:* (cf. p. 182) **19** *suspend sb.:* (cf p. 183) **29** *locker:* (cf. p. 182) **33–35** be second/first string (AE): be a substitute/regular player in a team **36** *pros = professionals:* professional football teams **37** *Steelers:* football team from Pittsburgh, Pennsylvania **40** *academic scholarship:* (cf. p. 181) **50** *incidentally:* übrigens • *"To Kill a Mockingbird":* American novel (1960) by Harper Lee (born 1926) about a Southern white lawyer defending a black man falsely accused of raping a white girl

I would tell you his position, but like I said, I would like to be anonymous to you. I hope you understand.

Love always,
Charlie

September 16, 1991

Dear friend,

I have finished *To Kill a Mockingbird*. It is now my favorite book of all time, but then again, I always think that until I read another book. My advanced english teacher asked me to call him "Bill" when we're not in class, and he gave me another book to read. He says that I have a great skill at reading and understanding language, and he wanted me to write an essay about *To Kill a Mockingbird*.

I mentioned this to my mom, and she asked why Bill didn't recommend that I just take a sophomore or junior english class. And I told her that Bill said that these were basically the same classes with more complicated books, and that it wouldn't help me. My mom said that she wasn't sure and would talk to him during open house. Then, she asked me to help her by washing the dishes, which I did.

Honestly, I don't like doing dishes. I like eating with my fingers and off napkins, but my sister says that doing so is bad for the environment. She is a part of the Earth Day Club here in high school, and that is where she meets the boys. They are all very nice to her, and I don't really understand why except maybe the fact that she is pretty. She really is mean to these boys.

One boy has it particularly hard. I won't tell you his name. But I will tell you all about him. He has very nice brown hair, and he wears it long with a ponytail. I think he will regret this when he looks back on his life. He is always making mix tapes for my sister with very specific themes. One was called "Autumn Leaves." He included many songs by the Smiths. He even hand-colored the cover. After the movie he rented was over, and he left, my sister gave me the tape.

"Do you want this, Charlie?"

I took the tape, but I felt weird about it because he had made it for her. But I listened to it. And loved it very much. There is one song called "Asleep" that I would like you to listen to. I told my sister about it. And a week later she thanked me because when this boy asked her about the tape, she said exactly what I said about the song "Asleep," and this boy was very moved by how much it meant to her. I hope this means I will be good at dating when the time comes.

I should stick to the subject, though. That is what my teacher Bill tells me to do because I write kind of the way I talk. I think that is why he wants me to write that essay about *To Kill a Mockingbird*.

This boy who likes my sister is always respectful to my parents. My mom likes him very much because of this. My dad thinks he's soft. I think that's why my sister does what she does to him.

This one night, she was saying very mean things about how he didn't stand up to the class bully when he was fifteen or something like that. To tell you the truth, I was just watching the movie he had rented, so I wasn't paying very close attention to their fight. They fight all the time, so I figured that the movie was at least something different, which it wasn't because it was a sequel.

Anyway, after she leaned into him for about four movie scenes, which I guess is about ten minutes or so, he started crying. Crying very hard. Then, I turned around, and my sister pointed at me.

"You see. Even Charlie stood up to his bully. You see."

And this guy got really red-faced. And he looked at me. Then, he looked at her. And he wound up and hit her hard across the face. I mean hard. I just froze because I couldn't believe he did it. It was not like him at all to hit anybody. He was the boy that made mix tapes with themes and hand-colored covers until he hit my sister and stopped crying.

The weird part is that my sister didn't do anything. She just looked at him very quietly. It was so weird. My sister goes crazy if you eat the wrong kind of tuna, but here was this guy hitting her, and she didn't

▷ **14** *sophomore/junior class:* (cf. pp. 183, 182) **28** *mix tape:* cassette tape that contains music from different sources **29** *"Autumn Leaves":* song (1946) written by the French poet Jacques Prevert and composer Joseph Kosma and translated into English by Johnny Mercer **30** *the Smiths:* British pop group of the 1980s, famous for their melancholic songs **47** *bully:* person who uses violence to force (usu. younger and weaker) people to do what he or she wants **51** *sequel:* movie that continues the story of an earlier one **52** *lean into sb.* (AE infml): be aggressive toward sb. **57** *wind up* [waɪnd] – *wound* [waʊnd] – *wound:* (here) get all your energy together

say anything. She just got soft and nice. And she asked me to leave, which I did. After the boy had left, she said that they were "going out" and not to tell mom or dad what happened.

I guess he stood up to his bully. And I guess that makes sense.

That weekend, my sister spent a lot of time with this boy. And they laughed a lot more than they usually did. On Friday night, I was reading my new book, but my brain got tired, so I decided to watch some television instead. And I opened the door to the basement, and my sister and this boy were naked.

He was on top of her, and her legs were draped over either side of the couch. And she screamed at me in a whisper.

"Get out. You pervert."

So, I left. The next day, we all watched my brother play football. And my sister invited this boy over. I am not sure when he left the previous night. They held hands and acted like everything was happy. And this boy said something about how the football team hasn't been the same since my brother graduated, and my dad thanked him. And when the boy left, my dad said that this boy was becoming a fine young man who could carry himself. And my mom was quiet. And my sister looked at me to make sure I wouldn't say anything. And that was that.

"Yes. He is." That's all my sister could say. And I could see this boy at home doing his homework and thinking about my sister naked. And I could see them holding hands at football games that they do not watch. And I could see this boy throwing up in the bushes at a party house. And I could see my sister putting up with it.

And I felt very bad for both of them.

Love always,
Charlie

September 18, 1991

Dear friend,

I never told you that I am in shop class, did I? Well, I am in shop class, and it is my favorite class next to Bill's advanced english class. I wrote the essay for *To Kill a Mockingbird* last night, and I handed it in to Bill this morning. We are supposed to talk about it tomorrow during lunch period.

The point, though, is that there is a guy in shop class named "Nothing." I'm not kidding. His name is "Nothing." And he is hilarious. "Nothing" got his name when kids used to tease him in middle school. I think he's a senior now. The kids started calling him Patty when his real name is Patrick. And "Nothing" told these kids, "Listen, you either call me Patrick, or you call me nothing."

So, the kids started calling him "Nothing." And the name just stuck. He was a new kid in the school district at the time because his dad married a new woman in this area. I think I will stop putting quotation marks around Nothing's name because it is annoying and disrupting my flow. I hope you do not find this difficult to follow. I will make sure to differentiate if something comes up.

So, in shop class Nothing started to do a very funny impersonation of our teacher, Mr. Callahan. He even painted in the muttonchop sideburns with a grease pencil. Hilarious. When Mr. Callahan found Nothing doing this near the belt sander, he actually laughed because Nothing wasn't doing the impersonation mean or anything. It was just that funny. I wish you could have been there because it was the hardest I've laughed since my brother left. My brother used to tell Polish jokes, which I know is wrong, but I just blocked out the Polish part and listened to the jokes. Hilarious.

Oh, incidentally, my sister asked for her "Autumn Leaves" mix tape back. She listens to it all the time now.

Love always,
Charlie

▷ **17** *graduate* (v): (cf. p. 182) **32** *shop class:* (cf. p. 183) **39** *hilarious:* very funny so that other people laugh a lot **47** *disrupt sth.:* interrupt sth. so that it is no longer fluent • *flow* (n): (here) ability to write continually **48** *differentiate:* (here) call attention to sth. that is different **49** *impersonation:* act of pretending to be a certain person **50–51** *muttonchop sideburns:* very thick hair growing down and outwards from the side of a man's face **51** *grease pencil:* type of pencil that makes thick black marks **52** *belt sander:* machine with which you can smooth wood, metal, etc.

September 29, 1991

Dear friend,

There is a lot to tell you about the last two weeks. A lot of it is good, but a lot of it is bad. Again, I don't know why this always happens.

First of all, Bill gave me a C on my *To Kill a Mockingbird* essay because he said that I run my sentences together. I am trying now to practice not to do that. He also said that I should use the vocabulary words that I learn in class like "corpulent" and "jaundice." I would use them here, but I really don't think they are appropriate in this format.

To tell you the truth, I don't know where they are appropriate to use. I'm not saying that you shouldn't know them. You should absolutely. But I just have never heard anyone use the words "corpulent" and "jaundice" ever in my life. That includes teachers. So, what's the point of using words nobody else knows or can say comfortably? I just don't understand that.

I feel the same way about some movie stars who are terrible to watch. Some of these people must have a million dollars at least, and yet, they keep doing these movies. They blow up bad guys. They yell at their detectives. They do interviews for magazines. Every time I see this one particular movie star on a magazine, I can't help but feel terribly sorry for her because nobody respects her at all, and yet they keep interviewing her. And the interviews all say the same thing.

They start with what food they are eating in some restaurant. "As ________ gingerly munched her Chinese Chicken Salad, she spoke of love." And all the covers say the same thing: "________ gets to the bottom of stardom, love, and his/her hit new movie/television show/album."

I think it's nice for stars to do interviews to make us think they are just like us, but to tell you the truth, I get the feeling that it's all a big lie. The problem is I don't know who's lying. And I don't know why these magazines sell as much as they do. And I don't know why the ladies in the dentist's office like them as much as they do. A Saturday ago, I was in the dentist's office, and I heard this conversation.

"Did you see that movie?" as she points to the cover.

"I did. I saw it with Harold."

"What do you think?"

"She is just lovely."

"Yeah. She is."

"Oh, I have this new recipe."

"Low-fat?"

"Uh-huh."

"Do you have some time tomorrow?"

"No. Why don't you have Mike fax it to Harold?"

"Okay."

Then, these ladies started talking about the one star I mentioned before, and they both had very strong opinions.

"I think it's disgraceful."

"Did you read the interview in *Good Housekeeping?*"

"A few months back?"

"Uh-huh."

"Disgraceful."

"Did you read the one in *Cosmopolitan?*"

"No."

"God, it was practically the same interview."

"I don't know why they give her the time of day."

The fact that one of these ladies was my mom made me feel particularly sad because my mom is beautiful. And she's always on a diet. Sometimes, my dad calls her beautiful, but she cannot hear him. Incidentally, my dad is a very good husband. He's just pragmatic.

After the dentist's office, my mom drove me to the cemetery where a lot of her relatives are buried. My dad does not like to go to the cemetery because it gives him the creeps. But I don't mind going at all because my Aunt Helen is buried there. My mom was always the pretty one, as they say, and my Aunt Helen was always the other one. The nice thing was my Aunt Helen was never on a diet. And my Aunt Helen was "corpulent." Hey, I did it!

My Aunt Helen would always let us kids stay up and watch *Saturday Night Live* when she was baby-sitting or when she was living with us and my parents went to another couple's house to get drunk and play board games. When I was very little, I remember going

▷ **5** *C:* (cf. p. 181) **8** *corpulent:* (of a person) fat • *jaundice* ['dʒɔːndɪs]: disease that causes the skin to become yellow **10** *format:* (here) type of text **25** *gingerly* ['dʒɪndʒəli]: in a careful way • *munch sth.:* eat sth. crisp in slow and steady way **63** *give sb. the creeps* (infml): make sb. feel scared **69** *"Saturday Night Live":* US comedy show **71** *board game:* Brettspiel

to sleep, while my brother and sister and Aunt Helen watched *Love Boat* and *Fantasy Island*. I could never stay awake when I was that little, and I wish I could, because my brother and sister talk about those moments sometimes. Maybe it's sad that these are now memories. And maybe it's not sad. And maybe it's just the fact that we loved Aunt Helen, especially me, and this was the time we could spend with her.

I won't start listing television episode memories, except one because I guess we're on the subject, and it seems like something everyone can relate to in a small way. And since I don't know you, I figure that maybe I can write about something that you can relate to.

The family was sitting around, watching the final episode of *M*A*S*H*, and I'll never forget it even though I was very young. My mom was crying. My sister was crying. My brother was using every ounce of strength he had not to cry. And my dad left during one of the final moments to make a sandwich. Now, I don't remember much about the program itself because I was too young, but my dad never left to make a sandwich except during commercial breaks, and then he usually just sent my mom. I walked to the kitchen, and I saw my dad making a sandwich ... and crying. He was crying harder than even my mom. And I couldn't believe it. When he finished making his sandwich, he put away the things in the refrigerator and stopped crying and wiped his eyes and saw me.

Then, he walked up, patted my shoulder, and said, "This is our little secret, okay, champ?"

"Okay," I said.

And Dad picked me up with the arm that wasn't holding the sandwich, and carried me to the room that had the television, and put me on his lap for the rest of the television episode. At the end of the episode, he picked me up, turned off the TV, and turned around.

And my dad declared, "That was a great series."

And my mom said, "The best."

And my sister asked, "How long was it on the air?"

And my brother replied, "Nine years, stupid."

And my sister responded, "You ... stupid."

And my dad said, "Stop it, right now."

And my mom said, "Listen to your father."

And my brother said nothing.

And my sister said nothing.

And years later I found out my brother was wrong.

I went to the library to look up the figures, and I found out that the episode we watched is the highest watched anything of television history, which I find amazing because it felt like just the five of us.

You know ... a lot of kids at school hate their parents. Some of them got hit. And some of them got caught in the middle of wrong lives. Some of them were trophies for their parents to show the neighbors like ribbons or gold stars. And some of them just wanted to drink in peace.

For me personally, as much as I don't understand my mom and dad and as much as I feel sorry for both of them sometimes, I can't help but love them very much. My mom drives to visit the cemetery of people she loves. My dad cried during *M*A*S*H*, and trusted me to keep his secret, and let me sit on his lap, and called me "champ."

Incidentally, I only have one cavity, and as much as my dentist asks me to, I just can't bring myself to floss.

Love always,
Charlie

October 6, 1991

Dear friend,

I feel very ashamed. I went to the high school football game the other day, and I don't know exactly why. In middle school, Michael and I would go to the games sometimes even though neither of us were popular enough to go. It was just a place to go on Fridays when we didn't want to watch television. Sometimes, we would see Susan there, and she and Michael would hold hands.

But this time, I went alone because Michael is gone, and Susan hangs around different boys now, and Bridget is still crazy, and Carl's mom sent him to a Catholic school, and Dave with the awkward glasses moved away. I was just kind of watching people, seeing who

▷ **13** *M*A*S*H:* TV series (1972–1983) about a mobile army surgical hospital during the Korean War (1950–1953) **54** *cavity:* hole in a tooth **55** *floss* (v): clean between the teeth with the help of a thin silk string

was in love and who was just hanging around, and I saw that kid I told you about. Remember Nothing? Nothing was there at the football game, and he was one of the few people who was not an adult that was actually watching the game. I mean really watching the game. He would yell things out.

"C'mon, Brad!" That's the name of our quarterback.

Now, normally I am very shy, but Nothing seemed like the kind of guy you could just walk up to at a football game even though you were three years younger and not popular.

"Hey, you're in my shop class!" He's a very friendly person.

"I'm Charlie." I said, not too shy.

"And I'm Patrick. And this is Sam." He pointed to a very pretty girl next to him. And she waved to me.

"Hey, Charlie." Sam had a very nice smile.

They both told me to have a seat, and they both seemed to mean it, so I took a seat. I listened to Nothing yell at the field. And I listened to his play-by-play analysis. And I figured out that this was a kid who knew football very well. He actually knew football as well as my brother. Maybe I should call Nothing "Patrick" from now on since that is how he introduced himself, and that is what Sam calls him.

Incidentally, Sam has brown hair and very very pretty green eyes. The kind of green that doesn't make a big deal about itself. I would have told you that sooner, but under the stadium lights, everything looked kind of washed out. It wasn't until we went to the Big Boy, and Sam and Patrick started to chain-smoke that I got a good look at her. The nice thing about the Big Boy was the fact that Patrick and Sam didn't just throw around inside jokes and make me struggle to keep up. Not at all. They asked me questions.

"How old are you, Charlie?"

"Fifteen."

"What do you want to do when you grow up?"

"I don't know just yet."

"What's your favorite band?"

"I think maybe the Smiths because I love their song 'Asleep,' but I'm really not sure one way or the other because I don't know any other songs by them too well."

"What's your favorite movie?"

"I don't know really. They're all the same to me."

"How about your favorite book?"

"*This Side of Paradise* by F. Scott Fitzgerald."

"Why?"

"Because it was the last one I read."

This made them laugh because they knew I meant it honest, not show-off. Then they told me their favorites, and we sat quiet. I ate the pumpkin pie because the lady said it was in season, and Patrick and Sam smoked more cigarettes.

I looked at them, and they looked really happy together. A good kind of happy. And even though I thought Sam was very pretty and nice, and she was the first girl I ever wanted to ask on a date someday when I can drive, I did not mind that she had a boyfriend, especially if he was a good guy like Patrick.

"How long have you been 'going out'?" I asked.

Then, they started laughing. Really laughing hard.

"What's so funny?" I said.

"We're brother and sister," Patrick said, still laughing.

"But you don't look alike," I said.

That's when Sam explained that they were actually stepsister and stepbrother since Patrick's dad married Sam's mom. I was very happy to know that because I would really like to ask Sam on a date someday. I really would. She is so nice.

I feel ashamed, though, because that night, I had a weird dream. I was with Sam. And we were both naked. And her legs were spread over the sides of the couch. And I woke up. And I had never felt that good in my life. But I also felt bad because I saw her naked without her permission. I think that I should tell Sam about this, and I really hope it does not prevent us from maybe making up inside jokes of our own. It would be very nice to have a friend again. I would like that even more than a date.

Love always,
Charlie

▷ **6** *quarterback:* position in American football **40** *"This Side of Paradise":* novel (1920) by the American author F. Scott Fitzgerald (1898–1940)

October 14, 1991

Dear friend,

Do you know what "masturbation" is? I think you probably do because you are older than me. But just in case, I will tell you. Masturbation is when you rub your genitals until you have an orgasm. Wow!

I thought that in those movies and television shows when they talk about having a coffee break that they should have a masturbation break. But then again, I think this would decrease productivity.

I'm only being cute here. I don't really mean it. I just wanted to make you smile. I meant the "wow" though.

I told Sam that I dreamt that she and I were naked on the sofa, and I started crying because I felt bad, and do you know what she did? She laughed. Not a mean laugh, either. A really nice, warm laugh. She said that she thought I was being cute. And she said it was okay that I had a dream about her. And I stopped crying. Sam then asked me if I thought she was pretty, and I told her I thought she was "lovely." Sam then looked me right in the eye.

"You know you're too young for me, Charlie? You do know that?"

"Yes, I do."

"I don't want you to waste your time thinking about me that way."

"I won't. It was just a dream."

Sam then gave me a hug, and it was strange because my family doesn't hug a lot except my Aunt Helen. But after a few moments, I could smell Sam's perfume, and I could feel her body against me. And I stepped back.

"Sam, I'm thinking about you that way."

She just looked at me and shook her head. Then, she put her arm around my shoulder and walked me down the hallway. We met Patrick outside because they didn't like to go to class sometimes. They preferred to smoke.

"Charlie has a Charlie-esque crush on me, Patrick."

"He does, huh?"

"I'm trying not to," I offered, which just made them laugh.

Patrick then asked Sam to leave, which she did, and he explained some things to me, so I would know how to be around other girls and not waste my time thinking about Sam that way.

"Charlie, has anyone told you how it works?"

"I don't think so."

"Well, there are rules you follow here not because you want to, but because you have to. You get it?"

"I guess so."

"Okay. You take girls, for example. They're copying their moms and magazines and everything to know how to act around guys."

I thought about the moms and the magazines and the everythings, and the thought made me nervous, especially if it includes TV.

"I mean it's not like in the movies where girls like assholes or anything like that. It's not that easy. They just like somebody that can give them a purpose."

"A purpose?"

"Right. You know? Girls like guys to be a challenge. It gives them some mold to fit in how they act. Like a mom. What would a mom do if she couldn't fuss over you and make you clean your room? And what would you do without her fussing and making you do it? Everyone needs a mom. And a mom knows this. And it gives her a sense of purpose. You get it?"

"Yeah," I said even though I didn't. But I got it enough to say "Yeah" and not be lying, though.

"The thing is some girls think they can actually change guys. And what's funny is that if they actually did change them, they'd get bored. They'd have no challenge left. You just have to give girls some time to think of a new way of doing things, that's all. Some of them will figure it out here. Some later. Some never. I wouldn't worry about it too much."

But I guess I did worry about it. I've been worrying about it ever since he told me. I look at people holding hands in the hallways, and I try to think about how it all works. At the school dances, I sit in the background, and I tap my toe, and I wonder how many couples will dance to "their song." In the hallways, I see the girls wearing the guys' jackets, and I think about the idea of property. And I wonder if anyone is really happy. I hope they are. I really hope they are.

Bill looked at me looking at people, and after class, he asked me what I was thinking about, and I told him. He listened, and he

▷ **9** *decrease sth.:* make sth. become less **10** *cute* (AE infml): clever in order to make a good impression **23** *hug* (n): act of putting your arms around sb. in a loving way **32** *have a crush on sb.:* in jdn. verknallt sein **51** *challenge:* Herausforderung **52** *mold:* pattern

nodded and made "affirmation" sounds. When I had finished, his face changed into a "serious talk" face.

"Do you always think this much, Charlie?"

"Is that bad?" I just wanted someone to tell me the truth.

"Not necessarily. It's just that sometimes people use thought to not participate in life."

"Is that bad?"

"Yes."

"I think I participate, though. Don't you think I am?"

"Well, are you dancing at these dances?"

"I'm not a very good dancer."

"Are you going on dates?"

"Well, I don't have a car, and even if I did, I can't drive because I'm fifteen, and anyway, I haven't met a girl I like except for Sam, but I am too young for her, and she would always have to drive, which I don't think is fair."

Bill smiled and continued asking me questions. Slowly, he got to "problems at home." And I told him about the boy who makes mix tapes hitting my sister because my sister only told me not to tell mom or dad about it, so I figured I could tell Bill. He got this very serious look on his face after I told him, and he said something to me I don't think I will forget this semester or ever.

"Charlie, we accept the love we think we deserve."

I just stood there, quiet. Bill patted my shoulder and gave me a new book to read. He told me everything was going to be okay.

I usually walk home from school because it makes me feel like I've earned it. What I mean is that I want to be able to tell my kids that I walked to school like my grandparents did in the "old days." It's odd that I'm planning this considering I've never had a date, but I guess that makes sense. It usually takes me an extra hour or so to walk as opposed to taking the bus, but it's worth it when the weather is nice and cool like it was today.

When I finally got home, my sister was sitting on a chair. My mom and my dad were standing in front of her. And I knew that Bill had called home and told them. And I felt terrible. It was all my fault.

My sister was crying. My mom was very very quiet. My dad did all the talking. He said that my sister was not allowed to see the boy who hit her anymore, and he was going to have a talk with the boy's parents tonight. My sister then said that it was all her fault, that she was provoking him, but my dad said it was no excuse.

"But I love him!" I had never seen my sister cry that much.

"No, you don't."

"I hate you!"

"No, you don't." My dad can be very calm sometimes.

"He's my whole world."

"Don't ever say that about anyone again. Not even me." That was my mom.

My mom chooses her battles carefully, and I can tell you one thing about my family. When my mom does say something, she always gets her way. And this time was no exception. My sister stopped crying immediately.

After that, my dad gave my sister a rare kiss on the forehead. Then, he left the house, got in his Oldsmobile, and drove away. I thought he probably was going to talk to the boy's parents. And I felt very sorry for them. His parents, I mean. Because my dad doesn't lose fights. He just doesn't.

My mom then went into the kitchen to make my sister's favorite thing to eat, and my sister looked at me.

"I hate you."

My sister said it different than she said it to my dad. She meant it with me. She really did.

"I love you," was all I could say in return.

"You're a freak, you know that? You've always been a freak. Everyone says so. They always have."

"I'm trying not to be."

Then, I turned around and walked to my room and closed my door and put my head under my pillow and let the quiet put things where they are supposed to be.

By the way, I figure you are probably curious about my dad. Did he hit us when we were kids or now even? I just thought you might be curious because Bill was, after I told him about that boy and my sister. Well, if you are wondering, he didn't. He never touched my brother or sister. And the only time he ever slapped me was when I made my Aunt Helen cry. And once we all calmed down, he got on his knees in

▷ **1** *affirmation:* meaning "yes"

front of me and said that his stepdad hit him a lot, and he decided in college when my mom got pregnant with my older brother that he would never hit his kids. And he felt terrible for doing it. And he was so sorry. And he would never hit me again. And he hasn't.

He's just stern sometimes.

Love always,
Charlie

October 15, 1991

Dear friend,

I guess I forgot to mention in my last letter that it was Patrick who told me about masturbation. I guess I also forgot to tell you how often I do it now, which is a lot. I don't like to look at pictures. I just close my eyes and dream about a lady I do not know. And I try not to feel ashamed. I never think about Sam when I do it. Never. That's very important to me because I was so happy when she said "Charlie-esque" since it felt like an inside joke of sorts.

One night, I felt so guilty that I promised God that I would never do it again. So, I started using blankets, but then the blankets hurt, so I started using pillows, but then the pillows hurt, so I went back to normal. I wasn't raised very religiously because my parents went to Catholic school, but I do believe in God very much. I just never gave God a name, if you know what I mean. I hope I haven't let Him down regardless.

Incidentally, my dad did have a serious talk with the boy's parents. The boy's mother was very very angry and screamed at her son. The boy's father kept quiet. And my dad didn't get too personal with them. He didn't tell them they did a "lousy job" raising their son or anything.

As far as he was concerned, the only important thing was getting their help to keep their son away from his daughter. Once that was settled, he left them to deal with their family and came home to deal with his. At least that's how he put it.

The one thing I did ask my dad was about the boy's problems at home. Whether or not he thought the parents hit their son. He told me to mind my own business. Because he didn't know and would never ask and didn't think it mattered.

"Not everyone has a sob story, Charlie, and even if they do, it's no excuse."

That's all he said. And then we went to watch television.

My sister is still mad at me, but my dad said I did the right thing. I hope that I did, but it's hard to tell sometimes.

Love always,
Charlie

October 28, 1991

Dear friend,

I'm sorry I haven't written to you in a couple of weeks, but I have been trying to "participate" like Bill said. It's strange because sometimes, I read a book, and I think I am the people in the book. Also, when I write letters, I spend the next two days thinking about what I figured out in my letters. I do not know if this is good or bad. Nevertheless, I am trying to participate.

Incidentally, the book Bill gave me was *Peter Pan* by J. M. Barrie. I know what you're thinking. The cartoon Peter Pan with the lost boys. The actual book is so much better than that. It's just about this boy who refuses to grow up, and when Wendy grows up, he feels very betrayed. At least that's what I got out of it. I think Bill gave me the book to teach me a lesson of some kind.

The good news is that I read the book, and because of its fantasy nature, I could not pretend that I was in the book. That way I could participate and still read.

In terms of my participation in things, I am trying to go to social events that they set up in my school. It's too late to join any clubs or

▷ **5** *stern:* very strict **23** *regardless:* anyway **27** *lousy* ['laʊzi] (infml): very bad **36** *sob story* (infml): part of your life that makes people feel sorry for you (*sob:* schluchzen) **51** *"Peter Pan":* famous British children's play (1904) and novel (1911) by J.M. Barrie (1860–1937) about a boy who refuses to grow older and lives in Neverland with other "lost boys"

anything like that, but I still try to go to the things that I can. Things like the homecoming football game and dance, even if I don't have a date.

I cannot imagine that I will ever come home for a homecoming game after I leave here, but it was fun to pretend that I was. I found Patrick and Sam sitting in their normal spot in the bleachers, and I started acting like I hadn't seen them in a year even though I had seen them that afternoon in lunch when I ate my orange, and they smoked cigarettes.

"Patrick, is that you? And Sam ... it's been so long. Who's winning? God, college is such a trial. My professor is making me read twenty-seven books this weekend, and my girlfriend needs me to paint signs for her protest rally Tuesday. Let those administrators know we mean business. Dad is busy with his golf swing, and Mom has her hands full with tennis. We must do this again. I would stay, but I have to pick my sister up from her emotional workshop. She's making real progress. Good to see ya."

And then I walked away. I went down to the concession stand and bought three boxes of nachos and a diet coke for Sam. When I returned, I sat down and gave Patrick and Sam the nachos and Sam her diet coke. And Sam smiled. The great thing about Sam is that she doesn't think I'm crazy for pretending to do things. Patrick doesn't either, but he was too busy watching the game and screaming at Brad, the quarterback.

Sam told me during the game that they were going over to their friend's house later for a party. Then, she asked me if I wanted to go, and I said yes because I had never been to a party before. I had seen one at my house, though.

My parents went to Ohio to see a very distant cousin get buried or married. I don't remember which. And they left my brother in charge of the house. He was sixteen at the time. My brother used the opportunity to throw a big party with beer and everything. I was ordered to stay in my room, which was okay because that's where everyone kept their coats, and it was fun looking through the stuff in their pockets. Every ten minutes or so, a drunk girl or boy would stumble in my room to see if they could make out there or something. Then, they would see me and walk away. That is, except for this one couple.

This one couple, whom I was told later were very popular and in love, stumbled into my room and asked if I minded them using it. I told them that my brother and sister said I had to stay here, and they asked if they could use the room anyway with me still in it. I said I didn't see why not, so they closed the door and started kissing. Kissing very hard. After a few minutes, the boy's hand went up the girl's shirt, and she started protesting.

"C'mon, Dave."

"What?"

"The kid's in here."

"It's okay."

And the boy kept working up the girl's shirt, and as much as she said no, he kept working it. After a few minutes, she stopped protesting, and he pulled her shirt off, and she had a white bra on with lace. I honestly didn't know what to do by this point. Pretty soon, he took off her bra and started to kiss her breasts. And then he put his hand down her pants, and she started moaning. I think they were both very drunk. He reached to take off her pants, but she started crying really hard, so he reached for his own. He pulled his pants and underwear down to his knees.

"Please. Dave. No."

But the boy just talked soft to her about how good she looked and things like that, and she grabbed his penis with her hands and started moving it. I wish I could describe this a little more nicely without using words like penis, but that was the way it was.

After a few minutes, the boy pushed the girl's head down, and she started to kiss his penis. She was still crying. Finally, she stopped crying because he put his penis in her mouth, and I don't think you can cry in that position. I had to stop watching at that point because I started to feel sick, but it kept going on, and they kept doing other things, and she kept saying "no." Even when I covered my ears, I could still hear her say that.

▷ **4** *homecoming:* (cf. p. 182) **6** *the bleachers* (AE): wooden seats at a sports stadium where the onlookers sit **18** *concession stand* (AE): the place at a sports event, etc. where a company has the right to sell sth. **36** *make out (with sb.)* (AE infml): kiss and touch sb. in a sexual way

My sister came in eventually to bring me a bowl of potato chips, and when she found the boy and the girl, they stopped. My sister was very embarrassed, but not as embarrassed as the girl. The boy looked kind of smug. He didn't say much. After they left, my sister turned to me.

"Did they know you were in here?"

"Yes. They asked if they could use the room."

"Why didn't you stop them?"

"I didn't know what they were doing."

"You pervert," was the last thing my sister said before she left the room, still carrying the bowl of potato chips.

I told Sam and Patrick about this, and they both got very quiet. Sam said that she used to go out with Dave for a while before she got into punk music, and Patrick said he heard about that party. I wasn't surprised that he did because it kind of became a legend. At least that's what I've heard when I tell some kids who my older brother is.

When the police came, they found my brother asleep on the roof. Nobody knows how he got there. My sister was making out in the laundry room with some senior. She was a freshman at the time. A lot of parents came to the house then to pick up their kids, and a lot of the girls were crying and throwing up. Most of the boys had run away by this point. My brother got in big trouble, and my sister was given a "serious talk" by my parents about bad influences. And that was that.

The boy named Dave is a senior now. He plays on the football team. He is a wide receiver. I watched the end of the game when Dave caught a touchdown thrown from Brad. It ended up winning the game for our school. And people went crazy in the stands because we won the game. But all I could think about was that party. I thought about it quiet for a long time, then I looked over to Sam.

"He raped her, didn't he?"

She just nodded. I couldn't tell if she was sad or just knew more things than me.

"We should tell someone, shouldn't we?"

Sam just shook her head this time. She then explained about all the things you have to go through to prove it, especially in high school when the boy and girl are popular and still in love.

The next day at the homecoming dance, I saw them dancing together. Dave and his girl. And I got really mad. It kind of scared me how mad I got. I thought about walking up to Dave and really hurting him like maybe I should have really hurt Sean. And I think I would have, but Sam saw me and put her arm around my shoulder like she does. She calmed me down, and I guess I'm glad she did because I think I would have gotten even madder if I started hitting Dave, and his girl stopped me because she loved him. I think I would have gotten even madder about that.

So, I decided to do the next best thing and let the air out of Dave's tires. Sam knew which was his car.

There is a feeling that I had Friday night after the homecoming game that I don't know if I will ever be able to describe except to say that it is warm. Sam and Patrick drove me to the party that night, and I sat in the middle of Sam's pickup truck. Sam loves her pickup truck because I think it reminds her of her dad. The feeling I had happened when Sam told Patrick to find a station on the radio. And he kept getting commercials. And commercials. And a really bad song about love that had the word "baby" in it. And then more commercials. And finally he found this really amazing song about this boy, and we all got quiet.

Sam tapped her hand on the steering wheel. Patrick held his hand outside the car and made air waves. And I just sat between them. After the song finished, I said something.

"I feel infinite."

And Sam and Patrick looked at me like I said the greatest thing they ever heard. Because the song was that great and because we all really paid attention to it. Five minutes of a lifetime were truly spent, and we felt young in a good way. I have since bought the record, and I would tell you what it was, but truthfully, it's not the same unless you're driving to your first real party, and you're sitting in the middle seat of a pickup with two nice people when it starts to rain.

We got to the house where the party was, and Patrick did this secret knock. It would be hard to describe to you this knock without sound. The door opened a crack, and this guy with frizzy hair looked out at us.

"Patrick known as Patty known as Nothing?"

"Bob."

▷ **25** *wide receiver:* player in an American football team **26** *touchdown:* (in American football) move that scores points **61** *infinite:* without limits, not having an end

The door opened, and the old friends hugged each other. Then, Sam and Bob hugged each other. Then, Sam spoke.

"This is our friend, Charlie."

And you won't believe it. Bob hugged me! Sam told me as we were hanging up our coats that Bob was "baked like a fucking cake." I really had to quote that one even though it has a swear.

The party was in the basement of this house. The room was quite smoky, and the kids were much older. There were two girls showing each other their tattoos and belly button rings. Seniors, I think.

This guy named Fritz something was eating a lot of Twinkies. Fritz's girlfriend was talking to him about women's rights, and he kept saying, "I know, baby."

Sam and Patrick started smoking cigarettes. Bob went up to the kitchen when he heard the bell ring. When he came back, he brought a can of Milwaukee's Best beer for everyone, as well as two new party guests. There was Maggie, who needed to use the bathroom. And there was Brad, the quarterback of the high school football team. No kidding!

I do not know why this excited me, but I guess when you see somebody in the hallway or on the field or something, it's nice to know that they are a real person.

Everyone was very friendly to me and asked me a lot of questions about myself. I guess because I was the youngest, and they didn't want me to feel out of place, especially after I said no to having a beer. I once had a beer with my brother when I was twelve, and I just didn't like it. It's really that simple for me.

Some of the questions I was asked was what grade I was in and what did I want to be when I grow up.

"I am a freshman, and I don't know just yet."

I looked around, and I saw that Sam and Patrick had left with Brad. That's when Bob started passing around food.

"Would you like a brownie?"

"Yes. Thank you."

I was actually quite hungry because normally Sam and Patrick take me to the Big Boy after the football games, and I guess I was used to it by now. I ate the brownie, and it tasted a little weird, but it was still a brownie, so I still liked it. But this was not an ordinary brownie. Since you are older, I think you know what kind of brownie it was.

After thirty minutes, the room started to slip away from me. I was talking to one of the girls with the belly button ring, and she seemed like she was in a movie. I started blinking a lot and looking around, and the music sounded heavy like water.

Sam came down and when she saw me, she turned to Bob.

"What the hell is your problem?"

"Come on, Sam. He likes it. Ask him."

"How do you feel, Charlie?"

"Light."

"You see?" Bob actually looked a little nervous, which I was later told was paranoia.

Sam sat down next to me and held my hand, which felt cool.

"Are you seeing anything, Charlie?"

"Light."

"Does it feel good?"

"Uh-huh."

"Are you thirsty?"

"Uh-huh."

"What would you like to drink?"

"A milkshake."

And everyone in the room, except Sam, erupted in laughter.

"He's stoned."

"Are you hungry, Charlie?"

"Uh-huh."

"What would you like to eat?"

"A milkshake."

I don't think they would have laughed any harder even if what I said was at all funny. Then, Sam took my hand and stood me up on the dizzy floor.

"C'mon. We'll get you a milkshake."

As we were leaving, Sam turned to Bob.

"I still think you're an asshole."

All Bob did was laugh. And Sam finally laughed, too. And I was glad that everyone seemed as happy as they seemed.

▷ **5** *baked* (sl): high on drugs **9** *belly button:* Bauchnabel **10** *Twinkie:* small cake filled with vanilla-creme **17–18** *No kidding!* (infml): honestly **29** *freshman:* (cf. p. 181) **32** *brownie:* type of chocolate cake cut into small rectangles **35** *Big Boy:* US fast-food chain

Sam and I got up to the kitchen, and she turned on the light. Wow! It was so bright, I couldn't believe it. It was like when you see a movie in the theater during the day, and when you leave the movie, you can't believe that it's still daylight outside. Sam got some ice cream and some milk and a blender. I asked her where the bathroom was, and she pointed around the corner almost like it was her house. I think she and Patrick spent a lot of time here when Bob was still in high school.

When I got out of the bathroom, I heard a noise in the room where we left our coats. I opened the door, and I saw Patrick kissing Brad. It was a stolen type of kissing. They heard me in the door and turned around. Patrick spoke first.

"Is that you, Charlie?"

"Sam's making me a milkshake."

"Who is this kid?" Brad just looked real nervous and not in the Bob way.

"He's a friend of mine. Relax."

Patrick then took me out of the room and closed the door. He put his hands on both of my shoulders and looked me straight in the eye.

"Brad doesn't want people to know."

"Why?"

"Because he's scared."

"Why?"

"Because he is ... wait ... are you stoned?"

"They said I was downstairs. Sam is making me a milkshake."

Patrick tried to keep from laughing.

"Listen, Charlie. Brad doesn't want people to know. I need you to promise that you won't tell anyone. This will be our little secret. Okay?"

"Okay."

"Thanks."

With that, Patrick turned around and went back into the room. I heard some muffled voices, and Brad seemed upset, but I didn't think it was any of my business, so I went back to the kitchen.

I have to say that it was the best milkshake I ever had in my life. It was so delicious, it almost scared me.

Before we left the party, Sam played me a few of her favorite songs. One was called "Blackbird." The other was called "MLK." They were both very beautiful. I mentioned the titles because they were as great when I listened to them sober.

Another interesting thing happened at the party before we left. Patrick came downstairs. I guess Brad had left. And Patrick smiled. And Bob started to make fun of him having a crush on the quarterback. And Patrick smiled more. I don't think I ever saw Patrick smile so much. Then, Patrick pointed at me, and said something to Bob.

"He's something, isn't he?"

Bob nodded his head. Patrick then said something I don't think I'll ever forget.

"He's a wallflower."

And Bob really nodded his head. And the whole room nodded their head. And I started to feel nervous in the Bob way, but Patrick didn't let me get too nervous. He sat down next to me.

"You see things. You keep quiet about them. And you understand."

I didn't know that other people thought things about me. I didn't know that they looked. I was sitting on the floor of a basement of my first real party between Sam and Patrick, and I remembered that Sam introduced me as her friend to Bob. And I remembered that Patrick had done the same for Brad. And I started to cry. And nobody in that room looked at me weird for doing it. And then I really started to cry.

Bob raised his drink and asked everyone to do the same.

"To Charlie."

And the whole group said, "To Charlie."

I didn't know why they did that, but it was very special to me that they did. Especially Sam. Especially her.

I would tell you more about the homecoming dance, but now that I'm thinking about it, me letting out the air of Dave's tires was the best part. I did try to dance like Bill suggested, but I usually like songs you can't dance to, so I didn't do it too much. Sam did look very pretty in her dress, but I was trying not to notice because I'm trying not to think of her that way.

I did notice that Brad and Patrick never talked once during the whole dance because Brad was off dancing with a cheerleader named

▷ **5** *blender:* Mixgerät, Mixer **38** *"Blackbird":* song (1968) by the Beatles • *"MLK":* song (1984) by U2

Nancy, who is his girlfriend. And I did notice that my sister was dancing with the boy she wasn't supposed to even though a different boy picked her up at the house.

After the dance, we left in Sam's pickup. Patrick was driving this time. As we were approaching the Fort Pitt Tunnel, Sam asked Patrick to pull to the side of the road. I didn't know what was going on. Sam then climbed in the back of the pickup, wearing nothing but her dance dress. She told Patrick to drive, and he got this smile on his face. I guess they had done this before.

Anyway, Patrick started driving really fast, and just before we got to the tunnel, Sam stood up, and the wind turned her dress into ocean waves. When we hit the tunnel, all the sound got scooped up into a vacuum, and it was replaced by a song on the tape player. A beautiful song called "Landslide." When we got out of the tunnel, Sam screamed this really fun scream, and there it was. Downtown. Lights on buildings and everything that makes you wonder. Sam sat down and started laughing. Patrick started laughing. I started laughing.

And in that moment, I swear we were infinite.

Love always,
Charlie

▷ **5** *Fort Pitt Tunnel:* tunnel in Pittsburgh **14** *"Landslide":* song (1975) by Fleetwood Mac

part 2

November 7, 1991

Dear friend,

It was one of those days that I didn't mind going to school because the weather was so pretty. The sky was overcast with clouds, and the air felt like a warm bath. I don't think I ever felt that clean before. When I got home, I had to mow the lawn for my allowance, and I didn't mind one bit. I just listened to the music, and breathed in the day, and remembered things. Things like walking around the neighborhood and looking at the houses and the lawns and the colorful trees and having that be enough.

I do not know anything about Zen or things that the Chinese or Indians do as part of their religion, but one of the girls from the party with the tattoo and belly button ring has been a Buddhist since July. She talks about very little else except maybe how expensive cigarettes are. I see her at lunch sometimes, smoking between Patrick and Sam. Her name is Mary Elizabeth.

Mary Elizabeth told me that the thing about Zen is that it makes you connected to everything in the world. You are part of the trees and the grass and the dogs. Things like that. She even explained how her tattoo symbolized this, but I can't remember how. So, I guess Zen is a day like this when you are part of the air and remember things.

One thing I remember is that the kids used to play a game. What you would do is take a football or something, and one person would have it, and all the other kids would try to tackle that kid. And then whoever got the ball next would run around with it, and the kids would try to tackle him. This could go on for hours. I never really understood the point of this game, but my brother loved it. He didn't like to run with the ball so much as he liked to tackle people. The kids called the game "smear the queer." I didn't really think about what that means until now.

Patrick told me the story about him and Brad, and now I understand why Patrick didn't get angry at Brad at the homecoming dance for dancing with a girl. When they were both juniors, Patrick and Brad were at a party together with the rest of the popular kids. Patrick actually used to be popular before Sam bought him some good music.

Patrick and Brad both got pretty drunk at this party. Actually, Patrick said that Brad was pretending to be a lot drunker than he really was. They were sitting in the basement with some girl named

Heather, and when she left to go to the bathroom, Brad and Patrick were left alone. Patrick said it was uncomfortable and exciting for both of them.

"You're in Mr. Brosnahan's class, right?"

"Have you ever gone to a *Pink Floyd* Laser Light Show?"

"Beer before liquor. Never sicker."

When they ran out of small talk, they just looked at each other. And they ended up fooling around right there in the basement. Patrick said it was like the weight of the whole world left both their shoulders.

But Monday in school, Brad kept saying the same thing.

"Man, I was so wasted. I don't remember a thing."

He said it to everyone who was at the party. He said it a few times to the same people. He even said it to Patrick. Nobody saw Patrick and Brad fool around, but Brad kept saying it anyway. That Friday, there was another party. And this time, Patrick and Brad got stoned although Patrick said that Brad was pretending to be a lot more stoned than he really was. And they ended up fooling around again. And Monday in school, Brad did the same thing.

"Man, I was so wasted. I don't remember a thing."

This went on for seven months.

It got to a point where Brad was getting stoned or drunk before school. It's not like he and Patrick were fooling around in school. They only fooled around at parties on Fridays, but Patrick said Brad couldn't even look at him in the hall, let alone speak with him. And it was hard, too, because Patrick really liked Brad.

When summer came, Brad didn't have to worry about school or anything, so his drinking and smoking got a lot worse. There was a big party at Patrick and Sam's house with the less than popular crowd. Brad showed up, which caused quite a stir because he was popular, but Patrick kept a secret as to why Brad came to the party. When most people left, Brad and Patrick went into Patrick's room.

They had sex for the first time that night.

▷ **6** *allowance* (AE): pocket money **24** *tackle sb.:* (in American football) try and take the ball away from sb. **29** *smear sb.:* flatten or beat up sb. • *queer:* (old-fashioned) person who is different; (derog sl) homosexual **43** *Pink Floyd:* British pop group (1966–1990s) **46** *fool around* (infml): (here) touch each other in a sexual way **50** *wasted* (sl): strongly affected by alcohol or drugs **68** *cause a stir:* Aufsehen erregen

I don't want to go into detail about it because it's pretty private stuff, but I will say that Brad assumed the role of the girl in terms of where you put things. I think that's pretty important to tell you. When they were finished, Brad started to cry really hard. He had been drinking a lot. And getting really really stoned.

No matter what Patrick did, Brad kept crying. Brad wouldn't even let Patrick hold him, which seems rather sad to me because if I have sex with someone, I would want to hold them.

Finally, Patrick just pulled up Brad's pants, and said to him.

"Just pretend you're passed out."

Then, Patrick got dressed and walked around the house to go into the party from a different direction than his bedroom. He was also crying pretty bad, and he decided if anyone asked him, he would say his eyes were red from smoking pot. Finally, he shook himself out of it and walked into the main party room. He acted really drunk. He went to Sam. "Have you seen Brad?" Sam saw the look in Patrick's eyes. Then, she spoke up to the party.

"Hey, has anyone seen Brad?"

Nobody at the party had, so a few people went to search for him. They finally found him in Patrick's room ... asleep.

Finally, Patrick called Brad's parents because he was really worried about him. He didn't tell them why, but he said that Brad was really sick at this party and needed to be taken home. Brad's parents did come, and Brad's father, along with some of the other boys including Patrick, carried Brad to the car.

Patrick doesn't know if Brad was really asleep or not at that point, but if he wasn't, it was a good acting job. Brad's parents sent him to rehabilitation because Brad's father didn't want him to miss his chance at a football scholarship. Patrick didn't see Brad for the rest of the summer.

Brad's parents never did figure out why their son was getting stoned and drunk all the time. Neither did anybody else. Except the people who knew.

When the school year started, Brad avoided Patrick a lot. He never went to the same parties as Patrick or anything until a little over a month ago. That was the night he threw rocks at Patrick's window and told Patrick that nobody could know, and Patrick understood. They only see each other now at night on golf courses and at parties like Bob's where the people are quiet and understand these things.

I asked Patrick if he felt sad that he had to keep it a secret, and Patrick just said that he wasn't sad because at least now, Brad doesn't have to get drunk or stoned to make love.

Love always,
Charlie

November 8, 1991

Dear friend,

Bill gave me my first B in advanced English class for my paper on *Peter Pan!* To tell you the truth, I don't know what I did differently from the other papers. He told me that my sense of language is improving along with my sentence structure. I think it's great that I could be improving on these things without noticing. By the way, Bill gives me A's on my report cards and letters to my parents. The grades on these papers are just between us.

I have decided that maybe I want to write when I grow up. I just don't know what I would write.

I thought about maybe writing for magazines just so I could see an article that didn't say things like I mentioned before. "As _________ wiped the honey mustard off of her lips, she spoke to me about her third husband and the healing power of crystals." But honestly, I think I would be a very bad reporter because I can't imagine sitting across the table from a politician or a movie star and asking them questions. I think I would probably just ask for their autograph for my mom or something. I would probably get fired for doing this. So, I thought about maybe writing for a newspaper instead because I could ask regular people questions, but my sister says that newspapers always lie. I do not know if this is true, so I'll just have to see when I get older.

▷ **10** *pass out* (infml): lose consciousness **14–15** *shake yourself out of it:* sich zusammenreißen

I did start working for a fanzine called *Punk Rocky*. It's this xerox magazine about punk rock and *The Rocky Horror Picture Show*. I don't write for it, but I help out.

Mary Elizabeth is in charge of it, just like she is in charge of the local *Rocky Horror Picture Show* showings. Mary Elizabeth is a very interesting person because she has a tattoo that symbolizes Buddhism and a belly button ring and wears her hair to make somebody mad, but when she's in charge of something, she acts like my dad when he comes home from a "long day." She is a senior, and she says that my sister is a tease and a snob. I told her not to say anything like that about my sister again.

Of all the things I've done this year so far, I think I like *The Rocky Horror Picture Show* the best. Patrick and Sam took me to the theater to see it on Halloween night. It's really fun because all these kids dress up like the people in the movie, and they act out the movie in front of the screen. Also, people shout at the movie on cue. I guess you probably know this already, but I thought I'd say it anyway in case you didn't.

Patrick plays "Frank 'N Furter." Sam plays "Janet." It is very hard to watch the movie because Sam walks around in her underwear when she plays Janet. I am really trying not to think of her that way, which is becoming increasingly difficult.

To tell you the truth, I love Sam. It's not a movie kind of love either. I just look at her sometimes, and I think she is the prettiest and nicest person in the whole world. She is also very smart and fun. I wrote her a poem after I saw her in *The Rocky Horror Picture Show*, but I didn't show it to her because I was embarrassed. I would write it out for you, but I think that would be disrespectful to Sam.

The thing is that Sam is now going out with a boy named Craig.

Craig is older than my brother. I think he may even be twenty-one because he drinks red wine. Craig plays "Rocky" in the show. Patrick says that Craig is "cut and hunky." I do not know where Patrick finds his expressions.

But I guess that he's right, Craig is cut and hunky. He is also a very creative person. He's putting himself through the Art Institute here by being a male model for JCPenney catalogs and things like that. He likes to take photographs, and I've seen a few of them, and they are very good. There is this one photograph of Sam that is just beautiful. It would be impossible to describe how beautiful it is, but I'll try.

If you listen to the song "Asleep," and you think about those pretty weather days that make you remember things, and you think about the prettiest eyes you've known, and you cry, and the person holds you back, then I think you will see the photograph.

I want Sam to stop liking Craig.

Now, I guess maybe you think that's because I am jealous of him. I'm not. Honest. It's just that Craig doesn't really listen to her when she talks. I don't mean that he's a bad guy because he's not. It's just that he always looks distracted.

It's like he would take a photograph of Sam, and the photograph would be beautiful. And he would think that the reason the photograph was beautiful was because of how he took it. If I took it, I would know that the only reason it's beautiful is because of Sam.

I just think it's bad when a boy looks at a girl and thinks that the way he sees the girl is better than the girl actually is. And I think it's bad when the most honest way a boy can look at a girl is through a camera. It's very hard for me to see Sam feel better about herself just because an older boy sees her that way.

I asked my sister about this, and she said that Sam has low self-esteem. My sister also said that Sam had a reputation when she was a sophomore. According to my sister, Sam used to be a "blow queen." I hope you know what that means because I really can't think about Sam and describe it to you.

I am really in love with Sam, and it hurts very much.

I did ask my sister about the boy at the dance. She wouldn't talk about it until I promised that I wouldn't tell anybody, not even Bill. So, I promised. She said that she has been seeing this boy secretly since Dad said she couldn't. She says she thinks about him when he's

▷ **1** *fanzine:* magazine for fans **1–2** *xerox magazine:* magazine that is photocopied **2** *"The Rocky Horror Picture Show":* film (1975) about a mad scientist called Dr. Frank 'N Furter, his creation "Rocky" and a couple called Brad and Janet, which developed a cult status with the audience dressing up and acting as characters from the film **10** *tease* (derog sl): woman who deliberately arouses men sexually without intending to satisfy them **16** *on cue:* (hier) an den richtigen Stellen **32** *cut and hunky* (sl): (here) big, strong and sexually attractive **35** *put sb. through sth. (e.g. college):* pay the expenses of sth. • *Art Institute:* Kunstakademie **36** *JCPenney:* US retailing company **48** *distracted:* geistesabwesend **58–59** *low self-esteem:* geringes Selbstwertgefühl **60** *blow queen* (derog sl): woman who likes to perform oral sex on men

not there. She says they're going to get married after they both finish college, and he finishes law school.

She told me not to worry because he hasn't hit her since that night. And she said not to worry because he won't hit her again. She really didn't say any more other than that, although she kept talking.

It was nice sitting with my sister that night because she almost never likes to talk to me. I was surprised that she told me as much as she did, but I guess that since she's keeping things secret, she can't tell anybody. And I guess she was just dying to tell somebody.

But as much as she told me not to, I do worry a lot about her. She is my sister, after all.

Love always,
Charlie

November 12, 1991

Dear friend,

I love Twinkies, and the reason I am saying that is because we are all supposed to think of reasons to live. In science class, Mr. Z. told us about an experiment where they got this rat or mouse, and they put this rat or mouse on one side of a cage. On the other side of the cage, they put a little piece of food. And this rat or mouse would walk over to the food and eat. Then, they put the rat or mouse back on its original side, and this time, they put electricity all through the floor where the rat or mouse would have to walk to get the piece of food. They did this for a while, and the rat or mouse stopped going to get the food at a certain amount of voltage. Then, they repeated the experiment, but they replaced the food with something that gave the rat or mouse intense pleasure. I don't know what it was that gave them intense pleasure, but I am guessing it is some kind of rat or mouse nip. Anyway, what the scientists found out was that the rat or mouse would put up with a lot more voltage for the pleasure. Even more than for the food.

I don't know the significance of this, but I find it very interesting.

Love always,
Charlie

November 15, 1991

Dear friend,

It's starting to get cold and frosty here. The pretty fall weather is pretty much gone. The good news is that we have holidays coming up, which I love especially now because my brother will be coming home soon. Maybe even for Thanksgiving! At least I hope he does for my mom.

My brother hasn't called home in a few weeks now, and Mom just keeps talking about his grades and sleeping habits and the foods he eats, and my dad keeps saying the same thing.

"He's not going to get injured."

Personally, I like to think my brother is having a college experience like they do in the movies. I don't mean the big fraternity party kind of movie. More like the movie where the guy meets a smart girl who wears a lot of sweaters and drinks cocoa. They talk about books and issues and kiss in the rain. I think something like that would be very good for him, especially if the girl were unconventionally beautiful. They are the best kind of girls, I think. I personally find "super models" strange. I don't know why this is.

My brother, on the other hand, has posters of "super models" and cars and beer and things like that on the walls in his room. I suppose if you add a dirty floor, it's probably what his dorm room looks like. My brother always hated making his bed, but he kept his clothes closet very organized. Go figure.

The thing is, when my brother does call home, he doesn't say a lot. He talks about his classes a little bit, but mostly he talks about the football team. There is a lot of attention on the team because they are very good, and they have some really big players. My brother said that one of the guys will probably be a millionaire someday, but that he is "dumb as a post." I guess that's pretty dumb.

My brother told this one story where the whole team was sitting around the locker room, talking about all the stuff they had to do to

▷ **29** *nip* (infml): small drink of strong alcohol **37** *fall* (n, AE): autumn **40** *Thanksgiving:* public holiday on the fourth Thursday in November, which is traditionally celebrated as a family reunion involving a big dinner with a turkey **47** *fraternity* (AE): (cf. p. 181) **49** *cocoa* ['koʊkoʊ]: hot chocolate drink **50** *issues:* important subjects **56** *dorm:* (cf. p. 181) **58** *Go figure:* Das soll einer verstehen! **64** *dumb as a post* (AE): strohdumm (*post:* Pfosten)

get into college football. They finally got around to talking about SAT scores, which I have never taken.

And this guy said, "I got a 710."

And my brother said, "Math or verbal?"

And the guy said, "Huh?"

And the whole team laughed.

I always wanted to be on a sports team like that. I'm not exactly sure why, but I always thought it would be fun to have "glory days." Then, I would have stories to tell my children and golf buddies. I guess I could tell people about *Punk Rocky* and walking home from school and things like that. Maybe these are my glory days, and I'm not even realizing it because they don't involve a ball.

I used to play sports when I was little, and I was actually very good, but the problem was that it used to make me too aggressive, so the doctors told my mom I would have to stop.

My dad had glory days once. I've seen pictures of him when he was young. He was a very handsome man. I don't know any other way to put it. He looked like all old pictures look. Old pictures look very rugged and young, and the people in the photographs always seem a lot happier than you are.

My mother looks beautiful in old pictures. She actually looks more beautiful than anyone except maybe Sam. Sometimes, I look at my parents now and wonder what happened to make them the way they are. And then I wonder what will happen to my sister when her boyfriend graduates from law school. And what my brother's face will look like on a football card, or what it will look like if it is never on a football card. My dad played college baseball for two years, but he had to stop when Mom got pregnant with my brother. That's when he started working at the office. I honestly don't know what my dad does.

He tells a story sometimes. It is a great story. It has to do with the state championship for baseball when he was in high school. It was the bottom of the ninth inning, and there was a runner on first. There were two outs, and my dad's team was behind by one run. My dad was younger than most of the varsity team because he was only a sophomore, and I think the team thought he was going to blow the game. He had all this pressure on him. He was really nervous. And really scared. But after a few pitches, he said he started feeling "in the zone." When the pitcher wound up and threw the next ball, he knew exactly where that ball was going to be. He hit it harder than any other ball he ever hit in his whole life. And he made a home run, and his team won the state championship. The greatest thing about this story is that every time my dad tells it, it never changes. He's not one to exaggerate.

I think about all this sometimes when I'm watching a football game with Patrick and Sam. I look at the field, and I think about the boy who just made the touchdown. I think that these are the glory days for that boy, and this moment will just be another story someday because all the people who make touchdowns and home runs will become somebody's dad. And when his children look at his yearbook photograph, they will think that their dad was rugged and handsome and looked a lot happier than they are.

I just hope I remember to tell my kids that they are as happy as I look in my old photographs. And I hope that they believe me.

Love always,
Charlie

November 18, 1991

Dear friend,

My brother finally called yesterday, and he can't make it home for any part of Thanksgiving weekend because he is behind on school because of football. My mom was so upset that she took me shopping for new clothes.

I know you think what I'm about to write is an exaggeration, but I promise you that it isn't. From the time we got into the car to the time we came home, my mom literally did not stop talking. Not once. Not even when I was in the dressing room trying on "slacks."

She just stood outside the dressing room and worried out loud. The things she said went all over the place. First, it was that my dad

▷ **1–2** *SAT scores:* (cf. p. 183) **8** *glory days:* a time in the past which people look back on as being better than the present **9** *buddy* (AE): friend **19** *rugged* ['rʌgɪd]: strong, attractive, manly **26** *football card:* card with the photograph of a famous football player, which is collected by fans **50** *yearbook* (AE): (cf. p. 183) **66** *slacks* (AE fml): trousers should've insisted that my brother come home if only for an afternoon. Then, it was that my sister had better start thinking more about her future and start applying to "safety" schools in case the good ones don't work out. And then she started saying that gray was a good color for me.

I understand how my mom thinks. I really do.

It's like when we were little, and we would go to the grocery store. My sister and brother would fight about things that my sister and brother would fight about, and I would sit at the bottom of the shopping cart. And my mom would be so upset by the end of shopping that she would push the cart fast, and I would feel like I was in a submarine.

Yesterday was like that except now I got to sit in the front seat.

When I saw Sam and Patrick at school today, they both agreed that my mom has very good taste in clothing. I told my mom this when I got home from school, and she smiled. She asked me if I wanted to invite Sam and Patrick over for dinner sometime after the holidays are over because my mom gets nervous enough as it is during the holidays. I called Sam and Patrick, and they said they would.

I'm really excited!

The last time I had a friend over to dinner was Michael last year. We had tacos. The really great part was that Michael stayed over to sleep. We ended up sleeping very little. We mostly just talked about things like girls and movies and music. The one part I remember distinctly was walking around the neighborhood at night. My parents were asleep along with the rest of the houses. Michael looked into all the windows. It was dark and quiet.

He said, "Do you think those people are nice?"

I said, "The Andersons? Yeah. They're old."

"What about those people?"

"Well, Mrs. Lambert doesn't like baseballs going into her yard."

"What about those people?"

"Mrs. Tanner has been visiting her mother for three months. Mr. Tanner spends his weekends sitting on the back porch and listening to baseball games. I don't really know if they're nice or not because they don't have children."

"Is she sick?"

"Is who sick?"

"Mrs. Tanner's mother."

"I don't think so. My mom would know, and she didn't say anything."

Michael nodded. "They're getting a divorce."

"You think so?"

"Uh-huh."

We just kept walking. Michael had a way of walking quiet sometimes. I guess I should mention that my mom heard that Michael's parents are divorced now. She said that only seventy percent of marriages stay together when they lose a child. I think she read it in a magazine somewhere.

Love always,
Charlie

November 23, 1991

Dear friend,

Do you enjoy holidays with your family? I don't mean your mom and dad family, but your uncle and aunt and cousin family? Personally, I do. There are several reasons for this.

First, I am very interested and fascinated by how everyone loves each other, but no one really likes each other. Second, the fights are always the same.

They usually start when my mom's dad (my grandfather) finishes his third drink. It is around this time that he starts to talk a lot. My grandfather usually just complains about black people moving into the old neighborhood, and then my sister gets upset at him, and then my grandfather tells her that she doesn't know what she's talking about because she lives in the suburbs. And then he says how no one visits him in his retirement home. And finally he starts talking about all of the family's secrets, like how cousin so-and-so "knocked up" that waitress from the Big Boy. I should probably mention that my

▷ **3** *"safety" schools:* (here) universities where a person is likely to get a place **22** *taco:* type of Mexican food **65** *the suburbs* (AE): residential areas outside a city centre, which in the USA are usually populated by whites **66** *retirement home:* old people's home **67** *knock sb. up* (AE sl): make sb. pregnant

grandfather can't hear very well, so he says all of these things really loud.

My sister tries to fight him, but she never wins. My grandfather is definitely more stubborn than she is. My mom usually helps her aunt prepare the food, which my grandfather always says is "too dry" even if it's soup. And her aunt will then cry and lock herself in the bathroom.

There is only one bathroom in my great aunt's house, so this turns to trouble when all the beer starts to hit my cousins. They stand twisted in bladder positions and bang on the door for a few minutes and almost coax my great aunt out, but then my grandfather curses something at my great aunt, and the cycle starts over again. With the exception of the one holiday when my grandfather passed out just after dinner, my cousins always have to go to the bathroom outside in the bushes. If you look out the windows like I do, you can see them, and it looks like they're on one of their hunting trips. I feel terribly sorry for my girl cousins and my other great aunts because they don't really have the bushes option, especially when it's cold.

I should mention that my dad usually just sits real quiet and drinks. My dad is not a big drinker at all, but when he has to spend time with my mom's family, he gets "loaded," as my cousin Tommy says. Deep down, I think my dad would rather spend the holiday with his family in Ohio. That way, he wouldn't have to be around my grandfather. He doesn't like my grandfather very much, but he keeps quiet about it. Even on the ride home. He just doesn't think it's his place.

As the evening comes to an end, my grandfather is usually too drunk to do much of anything. My dad and my brother and my cousins carry him out to the car of the person who is least angry at him. It has always been my job to open doors for them along the way. My grandfather is very fat.

I remember there was one time that my brother drove my grandfather back to the retirement home, and I rode along. My brother always understood my grandfather. He rarely got angry at him unless my grandfather said something mean about my mom or sister or made a scene in public. I remember it was snowing really hard, and it was very quiet. Almost peaceful. And my grandfather calmed down and started talking a different kind of talk.

He told us that when he was sixteen, he had to leave school because his dad died, and someone had to support the family. He talked about the time when he had to go to the mill three times a day to see if there was any work for him. And he talked about how cold it was. And how hungry he was because he made sure his family always ate before him. Things he said we just wouldn't understand because we were lucky. Then, he talked about his daughters, my mom and Aunt Helen.

"I know how your mom feels about me. I know Helen, too. There was one time ... I went to the mill ... no work ... none.... I came home at two in the morning ... pissed and pissed ... your grandmother showed me their report cards ... C-plus average ... and these were smart girls. So, I went into their room and I beat some sense into them ... and when it was done and they were crying, I just held up their report cards and said ... 'This will never happen again.' She still talks about it ... your mother ... but you know something ... it never did happen again ... they went to college ... both of them. I just wish I could have sent them ... I always wanted to send them... . I wish Helen could have understood that. I think your mother did ... deep down ... she's a good woman ... you should be proud of her."

When I told my mom about this, she just looked very sad because he could never say those things to her. Not ever. Not even when he walked her down the aisle.

But this Thanksgiving was different. It was my brother's football game, which we brought a VCR tape of for my relatives to watch. The whole family was gathered around the TV, even my great aunts, who never watch football. I'll never forget the looks on their faces when my brother took the field. It was a mixture of all things. My one cousin works in a gas station. And my other cousin has been out of work for two years since he injured his hand. And my other cousin has been wanting to go back to college for around seven years. And my dad said once that they were very jealous of my brother because he had a shot in life and was actually doing something about it.

But in that moment when my brother took the field, all that washed away, and everyone was proud. At one point, my brother

▷ **10** *twisted in bladder position:* gekrümmt mit zusammen gepressten Beinen **11** *coax sb. out:* gently persuade sb. to come out **21** *loaded* (AE infml): very drunk **40** *mill:* factory **48** *pissed* (AE): annoyed, angry **49** *report card:* (cf. p. 183) **60** *walk sb. (esp. a bride) down the aisle* [aɪl]: accompany sb. to the altar to marry the bridegroom **62** *VCR* (abbr, AE): video cassette recorder **66** *gas station* (AE): petrol station **69–70** *have a shot in life* (AE): have an opportunity to do sth. with your life

made a very big play on third down, and everyone cheered even though some of us had already seen the game before. I looked up at my dad, and he was smiling. I looked at my mom, and she was smiling even though she was nervous about my brother getting hurt, which was strange because it was a VCR tape of an old game, and she knew he didn't get hurt. My great aunts and my cousins and their children and everyone were also smiling. Even my sister. There were only two people who weren't smiling. My grandfather and I.

My grandfather was crying.

The kind of crying that is quiet and a secret. The kind of crying that only I noticed. I thought about him going into my mom's room when she was little and hitting my mom and holding up her report card and saying that her bad grades would never happen again. And I think now that maybe he meant my older brother. Or my sister. Or me. That he would make sure that he was the last one to work in a mill.

I don't know if that's good or bad. I don't know if it's better to have your kids be happy and not go to college. I don't know if it's better to be close with your daughter or make sure that she has a better life than you do. I just don't know. I was just quiet, and I watched him.

When the game was over and dinner was finished, everyone said what they were thankful for. A lot of it had to do with my brother or family or children or God. And everyone meant it when they said it regardless of what would happen tomorrow. When it came to my turn I thought about it a lot because this was my first time sitting at the big table with all the grown-ups since my brother wasn't here to take his seat.

"I'm thankful that my brother played football on television so nobody fought."

Most of the people around the table looked uncomfortable. Some looked angry. My dad looked like he knew I was right, but he didn't want to say anything because it wasn't his family. My mom was nervous about what her dad would do. Only one person at the table said anything. It was my great aunt, the one who usually locks herself in the bathroom.

"Amen."

And somehow that made it all right.

When we were all getting ready to leave, I walked up to my grandfather and gave him a hug and a kiss on the cheek. He wiped my lip print off with his palm and gave me a look. He doesn't like the boys in the family to touch him. But I'm very glad that I did it anyway in case he dies. I never got to do that with my Aunt Helen.

Love always,
Charlie

December 7, 1991

Dear friend,

Have you ever heard of a thing called "Secret Santa?" It's this activity where a group of friends draw names out of a hat, and they are supposed to buy a lot of Christmas presents for whatever person they choose. The presents are "secretly" placed in their lockers when they're not there. Then, at the end, you have a party, and all the people reveal who they really are as they give their last presents.

Sam started doing this with her group of friends three years ago. Now, it's some tradition. And supposedly the party at the end is always the best of the year. It happens the night after our last day of school before the break.

I don't know who got me. I got Patrick.

I'm really glad I got Patrick even though I wished for Sam. I haven't seen Patrick in a few weeks except in shop class because he has been spending most of his time with Brad, so thinking about presents is a good way to think about him.

The first present is going to be a mix tape. I just know that it should. I already have the songs picked and a theme. It's called "One Winter." But I've decided not to hand-color the cover. The first side has a lot of songs by the Village People and Blondie because Patrick likes that type of music a lot. It also has "Smells Like Teen Spirit" by Nirvana, which Sam and Patrick love. But the second side is the one I like the most. It has winter kind of songs.

▷ **64** *Village People:* disco group of the 1970s, famous for songs like "YMCA" • *Blondie:* new wave band (1978–1982) **65** *Nirvana:* US grunge band (1988– 1994)

Here they are:

Asleep by the Smiths
Vapour Trail by Ride
Scarborough Fair by Simon & Garfunkel
A Whiter Shade of Pale by Procol Harum
Time of No Reply by Nick Drake
Dear Prudence by the Beatles
Gypsy by Suzanne Vega
Nights in White Satin by the Moody Blues
Daydream by Smashing Pumpkins
Dusk by Genesis (before Phil Collins was even in the band!)
MLK by U2
Blackbird by the Beatles
Landslide by Fleetwood Mac

And finally …
Asleep by the Smiths (again!)

I spent all night working on it, and I hope Patrick likes it as much as I do. Especially the second side. I hope it's the kind of second side that he can listen to whenever he drives alone and feel like he belongs to something whenever he's sad. I hope it can be that for him.

I had an amazing feeling when I finally held the tape in my hand. I just thought to myself that in the palm of my hand, there was this one tape that had all of these memories and feelings and great joy and sadness. Right there in the palm of my hand. And I thought about how many people have loved those songs. And how many people got through a lot of bad times because of those songs. And how many people enjoyed good times with those songs. And how much those songs really mean. I think it would be great to have written one of those songs. I bet if I wrote one of them, I would be very proud. I hope the people who wrote those songs are happy. I hope that they feel it's enough. I really do because they've made me happy. And I'm only one person.

I can't wait to get my driver's license. It's coming up soon!

Incidentally, I have not told you about Bill in a while. But I guess there's not a lot to tell because he just keeps giving me books that he doesn't give his other students, and I keep reading them, and he keeps asking me to write papers, and I do. In the last month or so, I have read *The Great Gatsby* and *A Separate Peace*. I am starting to see a real trend in the kind of books Bill gives me to read. And just like the tape of songs, it is amazing to hold each of them in the palm of my hand. They are all my favorites. All of them.

Love always,
Charlie

December 11, 1991

Dear friend,

Patrick loved the tape! I think he knows that I'm his Secret Santa, though, because I think he knows that only I would do a tape like that. He also knows what my handwriting looks like. I don't know why I don't think of these things until it's too late. I really should have saved it for my last present.

Incidentally, I have thought of my second gift for Patrick. It is magnetic poetry. Have you heard of this? In case you haven't, I will explain. Some guy or girl put a whole bunch of words on a sheet of magnet and then cut the words into separate pieces. You put them on your refrigerator, and then you write poems while you make a sandwich. It's very fun.

The gift from my Secret Santa wasn't anything special. That makes me sad. I bet you anything that Mary Elizabeth is my Secret Santa because only she would give me socks.

Love always,
Charlie

▷ **38** "*The Great Gatsby*": novel (1925) by F. Scott Fitzgerald (cf. p. 23) • "*A Separate Peace*": novel (1960) by John Knowles (born 1926)

December 19, 1991

Dear friend,

I have since received thrift store "slacks." I have also received a tie, a white shirt, shoes, and an old belt. I'm guessing that my last gift at the party will be a suit coat because it's the only thing left. I was told by a typed note to wear everything I had been given to the party. I hope there is something behind this.

The good news is that Patrick liked all my gifts very much. Gift number three was a set of watercolor paints and some paper. I thought he might like to get them even if he never uses them. Gift number four was a harmonica and a book about playing it. I guess it's probably the same gift as the water colors, but I really think that everyone should have watercolors, magnetic poetry, and a harmonica.

My last gift before the party is a book called *The Mayor of Castro Street*. It is about a man named Harvey Milk, who was a gay leader in San Francisco. I went to the library when Patrick told me he was gay, and I did some research because I honestly didn't know much about it. I found an article about a documentary movie about Harvey Milk. And when I couldn't find the movie, I just searched for his name, and I found this book.

I have not read it myself, but the description on the book seemed very good. I hope that it means something to Patrick. I can't wait for the party, so I can give Patrick my party present. Incidentally, I have taken all my finals for the semester, and it has been very busy, and I would have told you all about it, but it just doesn't seem as interesting as these other things that have to do with holidays.

Love always,
Charlie

December 21, 1991

Dear friend,

Wow. Wow. I can paint the picture for you if you like. We are all sitting in Sam and Patrick's house, which I had never seen before. It was a rich house. Very clean. And we were all giving our final presents. The outside lights were on, and it was snowing, and it looked like magic. Like we were somewhere else. Like we were someplace better.

It was the first time I had ever met Sam and Patrick's parents. They were so nice. Sam's mom is very pretty and tells great jokes. Sam said she used to be an actress when she was younger. Patrick's dad is very tall and has a great handshake. He is also a very good cook. A lot of parents make you feel very awkward when you meet them. But not Sam and Patrick's. They were friendly all through dinner, and when dinner was over, they left so we could have our party. They didn't even check on us or anything. Not once. They just let us pretend it was our house. So, we decided to have the party in the "games" room, which had no games but a great rug.

When I revealed that I was Patrick's Secret Santa, everyone laughed because everyone knew, and Patrick did his best impersonation of being surprised, which was nice of him. Then, everyone asked what my last gift was, and I told them it was a poem I read a long time ago. It was a poem that Michael made a copy of for me. And I have read it a thousand times since because I don't know who wrote it. I don't know if it was ever in a book or a class. And I don't know how old the person was. But I know that I want to know him or her. I want to know that this person is okay.

So, everyone asked me to stand up and read the poem. And I wasn't shy because we were trying to act like grown-ups, and we drank brandy. And I was warm. I'm still a little warm, but I have to tell you this. So, I stood up, and just before I read this poem, I asked everyone if they knew who wrote it to please tell me.

When I was done reading the poem, everyone was quiet. A very sad quiet. But the amazing thing was that it wasn't a bad sad at all. It was just something that made everyone look around at each other and know that they were there. Sam and Patrick looked at me. And I looked at them. And I think they knew. Not anything specific really. They just knew. And I think that's all you can ever ask from a friend.

▷ **3** *thrift store:* Secondhandladen **16** *Harvey Milk* (1930–1978): gay activist and politician who (together with the mayor of San Francisco) was shot dead for promoting gay equality **25** *finals:* (cf. p. 181) **49–50** *do an impersonation of sth.:* pretend to feel/be sth.

That's when Patrick put on the second side of the tape I made for him and poured everyone another glass of brandy. I guess we all looked a little silly drinking it, but we didn't feel silly. I can tell you that.

As the songs kept playing, Mary Elizabeth stood up. But she wasn't holding a suit coat. It turns out that she wasn't my Secret Santa at all. She was the Secret Santa to the other girl with the tattoo and belly button ring, whose real name is Alice. She gave her some black nail polish that Alice had had her eye on. And Alice was very grateful. I just sat there, looking around the room. Looking for the suit coat. Not knowing who could possibly be holding it.

Sam stood up next, and she gave Bob a handcrafted Native American marijuana pipe, which seemed appropriate.

More people gave more gifts. And more hugs were exchanged. And finally, it came to the end. No one was left except for Patrick. And he stood up and walked into the kitchen.

"Does anyone want any chips?"

Everyone did. And he came out with three tubes of Pringles and a suit coat. And he walked up to me. And he said that all the great writers used to wear suits all the time.

So, I put on the suit even though I didn't feel like I really deserved to since all I write are essays for Bill, but it was such a nice present, and everyone clapped their hands anyway. Sam and Patrick both agreed I looked handsome. Mary Elizabeth smiled. I think it was the first time in my life I ever felt like I looked "good." Do you know what I mean? That nice feeling when you look in the mirror, and your hair's right for the first time in your life? I don't think we should base so much on weight, muscles, and a good hair day, but when it happens, it's nice. It really is.

The rest of the evening was very special. Since a lot of people were going away with their families to places like Florida and Indiana, we all exchanged presents with the people we weren't Secret Santas for.

Bob gave Patrick an eighth of marijuana with a Christmas card attached. He even wrapped it. Mary Elizabeth gave Sam earrings. So did Alice. And Sam gave them earrings, too. I think that is a private girl thing. I have to admit, I felt a little sad because other than Sam and Patrick, nobody got me a present. I guess I'm not that close with them, so it makes sense. But I still felt a little sad.

And then it came to my turn. I gave Bob a little plastic tube of soap bubbles because it just seemed to fit his personality. I guess I was right.

"Too much," was all he said.

He spent the rest of the night blowing bubbles at the ceiling.

Next was Alice. I gave her a book by Anne Rice because she is always talking about her. And she looked at me like she couldn't believe I knew she loved Anne Rice. I guess she didn't know how much she talked or how much I listen. But she thanked me all the same. Next came Mary Elizabeth. I gave her forty dollars inside a card. The card said something pretty simple: "To be spent on printing *Punk Rocky* in color next time."

And she looked at me funny. Then, they all started to look at me funny except for Sam and Patrick. I think they started feeling bad because they didn't get me anything. But I don't think they should have because I don't think that's the point really. Mary Elizabeth just smiled, and said thanks, and then stopped looking at me in the eye.

Last came Sam. I had been thinking about this present for a long time. I think I thought about this present from the first time I really saw her. Not met her or saw her but the first time I really saw her if you know what I mean. There was a card attached.

Inside the card, I told Sam that the present I gave her was given to me by my Aunt Helen. It was an old 45 record that had the Beatles' song "Something." I used to listen to it all the time when I was little and thinking about grown-up things. I would go to my bedroom window and stare at my reflection in the glass and the trees behind it and just listen to the song for hours. I decided then that when I met someone I thought was as beautiful as the song, I should give it to that person. And I didn't mean beautiful on the outside. I meant beautiful in all ways. So, I was giving it to Sam.

Sam looked at me soft. And she hugged me. And I closed my eyes because I wanted to know nothing but her arms. And she kissed my cheek and whispered so nobody could hear.

"I love you."

▷ **44** *Anne Rice* (born 1941): American novelist, author of *The Vampire Chronicles* (e.g. *Interview with the Vampire*)

I knew that she meant it in a friend way, but I didn't care because it was the third time since my Aunt Helen died that I heard it from anyone. The other two times were from my mom.

After that, I couldn't believe that Sam actually got me a present because I honestly thought that the "I love you" was it. But she did get me a present. And for the first time, something nice like that made me smile and not cry. I guess Sam and Patrick went to the same thrift store because their gifts went together. She took me to her room and stood me in front of her dresser, which was covered in a pillowcase with pretty colors. She lifted off the pillowcase, and there I was, standing in my old suit, looking at an old typewriter with a fresh ribbon. Inside the typewriter was a piece of white paper.

On that piece of white paper, Sam wrote, "Write about me sometime." And I typed something back to her, standing right there in her bedroom. I just typed.

"I will."

And I felt good that those were the first two words that I ever typed on my new old typewriter that Sam gave me. We just sat there quiet for a moment, and she smiled. And I moved to the typewriter again, and I wrote something.

"I love you, too."

And Sam looked at the paper, and she looked at me.

"Charlie ... have you ever kissed a girl?"

I shook my head no. It was so quiet.

"Not even when you were little?"

I shook my head no again. And she looked very sad.

She told me about the first time she was kissed. She told me that it was with one of her dad's friends. She was seven. And she told nobody about it except for Mary Elizabeth and then Patrick a year ago. And she started to cry. And she said something that I won't forget. Ever.

"I know that you know that I like Craig. And I know that I told you not to think of me that way. And I know that we can't be together like that. But I want to forget all those things for a minute. Okay?"

"Okay."

"I want to make sure that the first person you kiss loves you. Okay?"

"Okay." She was crying harder now. And I was, too, because when I hear something like that I just can't help it.

"I just want to make sure of that. Okay?"

"Okay."

And she kissed me. It was the kind of kiss that I could never tell my friends about out loud. It was the kind of kiss that made me know that I was never so happy in my whole life.

Once on a yellow piece of paper with green lines
he wrote a poem
And he called it "Chops"
because that was the name of his dog
And that's what it was all about
And his teacher gave him an A
and a gold star
And his mother hung it on the kitchen door
and read it to his aunts
That was the year Father Tracy
took all the kids to the zoo
And he let them sing on the bus
And his little sister was born
with tiny toenails and no hair
And his mother and father kissed a lot
And the girl around the corner sent him a
Valentine signed with a row of X's
and he had to ask his father what the X's meant
And his father always tucked him in bed at night
And was always there to do it

Once on a piece of white paper with blue lines
he wrote a poem
And he called it "Autumn"
because that was the name of the season
And that's what it was all about
And his teacher gave him an A
and asked him to write more clearly
And his mother never hung it on the kitchen door
because of its new paint

▷ **9** *dresser* (AE): Kommode **63** *tuck sb. in* (usu. *into*) *bed:* make sb. feel comfortable in bed by pulling the covers up around him or her

And the kids told him
that Father Tracy smoked cigars
And left butts on the pews
And sometimes they would burn holes
That was the year his sister got glasses
with thick lenses and black frames
And the girl around the corner laughed
when he asked her to go see Santa Claus
And the kids told him why
his mother and father kissed a lot
And his father never tucked him in bed at night
And his father got mad
when he cried for him to do it.

Once on a paper torn from his notebook
he wrote a poem
And he called it "Innocence: A Question"
because that was the question about his girl
And that's what it was all about
And his professor gave him an A
and a strange steady look
And his mother never hung it on the kitchen door
because he never showed her
That was the year that Father Tracy died
And he forgot how the end
of the Apostles' Creed went
And he caught his sister
making out on the back porch
And his mother and father never kissed
or even talked
And the girl around the corner
wore too much makeup
That made him cough when he kissed her
but he kissed her anyway
because that was the thing to do
And at three A.M. he tucked himself into bed
his father snoring soundly

That's why on the back of a brown paper bag
he tried another poem
And he called it "Absolutely Nothing"
Because that's what it was really all about
And he gave himself an A
and a slash on each damned wrist
And he hung it on the bathroom door
because this time he didn't think
he could reach the kitchen.

That was the poem I read for Patrick. Nobody knew who wrote it, but Bob said he heard it before, and he heard that it was some kid's suicide note. I really hope it wasn't because then I don't know if I like the ending.

Love always,
Charlie

December 23, 1991

Dear friend,

Sam and Patrick left with their family for the Grand Canyon yesterday. I don't feel too bad about it because I can still remember Sam's kiss. It feels peaceful and right. I even considered not washing my lips like they do on TV, but then I thought it would get too gross. So, instead I spent today walking around the neighborhood. I even got out my old sled and my old scarf. There is something cozy about that for me.

I walked over to the hill where we used to go and sled. There were a lot of little kids there. I watched them flying. Doing jumps and having races. And I thought that all those little kids are going to grow up someday. And all of those little kids are going to do the things that we do. And they will all kiss someone someday. But for now, sledding

▷ **3** *butt:* cigarette or cigar end • *pew:* wooden bench in a church **25** *the Apostles' Creed:* das Apostolische Glaubensbekenntnis **42** *slash* (n): sharp movement made with a knife • *wrist:* the joint between the hand and the arm **57** *gross* [grous]: disgusting, unpleasant **59** *sled* (BE: *sledge*): Schlitten • *cozy* (BE: *cosy*): (here) comforting

is enough. I think it would be great if sledding were always enough, but it isn't.

I'm really glad that Christmas and my birthday are soon because that means they will be over soon because I can already feel myself going to a bad place I used to go. After my Aunt Helen was gone, I went to that place. It got so bad that my mom had to take me to a doctor, and I was held back a grade. But now I'm trying not to think about it too much because that makes it worse.

It's kind of like when you look at yourself in the mirror and you say your name. And it gets to a point where none of it seems real. Well, sometimes, I can do that, but I don't need an hour in front of a mirror. It happens very fast, and things start to slip away. And I just open my eyes, and I see nothing. And then I start to breathe really hard trying to see something, but I can't. It doesn't happen all the time, but when it does, it scares me.

It almost happened this morning, but I thought of Sam's kiss, and it went away.

I probably shouldn't be writing about this too much because it brings it up too much. It makes me think too much. And I am trying to participate. It's just hard because Sam and Patrick are in the Grand Canyon.

Tomorrow, I'm going with my mom to buy presents for everyone. And then we are celebrating my birthday. I was born on December 24. I don't know if I ever told you that. It's a strange birthday to have because it is so close to Christmas. After that, we are celebrating Christmas with my dad's family, and my brother will be home for a little while. Then, I'm going out to take my driver's test, so I will be busy while Sam and Patrick are gone.

Tonight, I watched some television with my sister, but she didn't want to watch the Christmas specials that were on, so I decided to go upstairs and read.

Bill gave me one book to read over the break. It's *The Catcher in the Rye*. It was Bill's favorite book when he was my age. He said it was the kind of book you made your own.

I read the first twenty pages. I don't know how I feel about it just yet, but it does seem appropriate to this time. I hope Sam and Patrick call on my birthday. It would make me feel much better.

Love always,
Charlie

December 25, 1991

Dear friend,

I am sitting in my dad's old bedroom in Ohio. The family is still downstairs. I really don't feel very well. I don't know what's wrong with me, but I'm starting to get scared. I wish we were going back home tonight, but we always sleep over. I don't want to tell my mom about it because it would just make her worry. I would tell Sam and Patrick, but they didn't call yesterday. And we left this morning after we opened presents. Maybe they called this afternoon. I hope they didn't call this afternoon because I wasn't there. I hope it's okay that I'm telling you this. I just don't know what else to do. I always get sad when this happens, and I wish Michael were here. And I wish my Aunt Helen were here. I miss my Aunt Helen like this. Reading the book isn't helping either. I don't know. I'm just thinking too fast. Much too fast. It's like tonight.

The family watched *It's a Wonderful Life*, which is a very beautiful movie. And all I could think was why didn't they make the movie about Uncle Billy? George Bailey was an important man in the town. Because of him, a whole bunch of people got to get out of the slums. He saved a town, and when his dad died, he was the only guy who could do it. He wanted to live an adventure, but he stayed behind and sacrificed his dreams for the better good of the community. And then when that made him sad, he was going to kill himself. He was going to die because his life insurance money would have taken care of his family. And then an angel comes down and shows him what life would be if he had never been born. How the whole town would have suffered. And how his wife would have been an "old maid." And my sister didn't even say anything about how that's such an old-fashioned thing, this year. Every other year she says something about how Mary was working for a living, and just because she's not married, it doesn't mean that she is worthless. But this year she didn't. I didn't know why. I thought it might be about that secret boy of hers. Or maybe it's what happened in the car on the way over to our grandma's house. I just wanted the movie to be about Uncle Billy

▷ **7** *be held back a grade:* repeat a year **31–32** *"The Catcher in the Rye":* novel (1951) by J.D. Salinger (born 1919) **35** *appropriate* [ə'proupriət]: passend, angemessen **54** *It's a Wonderful Life:* film (1946)

because he drank a lot and was fat and lost the money in the first place. I wanted the angel to come down and show us how Uncle Billy's life had meaning. Then, I think I'd feel better.

It started yesterday at home. I don't like my birthday. I don't like it at all. I went shopping with my mom and sister, and my mom was in a bad mood because of parking spaces and lines. And my sister was in a bad mood because she couldn't buy her secret boy a present and hide it from Mom. She would have to come back herself later. And I felt weird. Really weird, because as I was walking around all the stores, I didn't know what present my dad would like to receive from me. I knew what to buy or give Sam and Patrick, but I didn't know what I could buy or give or make for my own dad. My brother likes posters of girls and beer cans. My sister likes a haircut gift certificate. My mom likes old movies and plants. My dad only likes golf, and that is not a winter sport except for in Florida, and we don't live there. And he doesn't play baseball anymore. He doesn't like to be even reminded unless he tells the stories. I just wanted to know what to buy my dad because I love him. And I don't know him. And he doesn't like to talk about things like that.

"Well, why don't you chip in with your sister and buy him that sweater?"

"I don't want to. I want to buy him something. What kind of music does he like?"

My dad doesn't listen to music a lot anymore, and the stuff he likes, he has.

"What kind of books does he like to read?"

My dad doesn't read books too much anymore because he listens to books on cassette tapes on the way to work, and he gets them free from the library.

What kind of movies? What kind of anything?

My sister decided to buy the sweater on her own. And she started to get mad at me because she needed time to come back to the store to buy that present for her secret boyfriend.

"Just buy him some golf balls, Charlie. Jesus."

"But that's a summer sport."

"Mom. Would you make him buy something?"

"Charlie. Calm down. It's okay."

I felt so sad. I didn't know what was going on. Mom was trying to be really nice because when I get like this, she is the one that tries real hard to keep things calm.

"I'm sorry, Mom."

"No. Don't be sorry. You want to get a nice present for your father. That's a good thing."

"Mom!" My sister was really getting mad.

My mom didn't even look at my sister.

"Charlie, you can buy your father whatever you want. I know he'll love it. Now, calm down. It's okay."

My mom took me to four different stores. Each one my sister just sat in the nearest chair and groaned. I finally found the perfect store. It was a movie place. And I found a videocassette of the last episode of *M*A*S*H* without the commercials. And I felt a lot better. Then, I started telling Mom about how we all watched it together.

"She knows, Charlie. She was there. Let's go. Duh."

My mom told my sister to mind her own business, and she listened to me tell the story that she already knew, leaving out the part about my dad crying because that was our little secret. My mom even told me how I tell stories very well. I love my mom. And this time, I told her I loved her. And she told me she loved me, too. And things were okay for a little while.

We were sitting at the dinner table, waiting for my dad to come home with my brother from the airport. He was really late, and my mom started to worry because it was snowing really hard outside. And she kept my sister at home because she needed help with dinner. She wanted it to be extra special for my brother and for me because he was coming home, and it was my birthday. But my sister just wanted to buy her boyfriend a present. She was in a really bad mood. She was being like those bratty girls in movies from the 1980s, and my mom kept saying "Young lady" after every sentence.

My dad finally called and said that because of the snow, my brother's plane was going to be very late. I just heard my mom's side of the discussion.

▷ **6** *line* (BE: *queue*): Warteschlange **9** *weird* [wɪrd; BE wɪəd]: strange **20** *chip in with sb.:* give money together with sb. to get sth. **53** *duh:* expression to show sb. that you think he or she is stupid **67** *bratty:* badly-behaved

"But it's Charlie's birthday dinner ... I don't expect you to do anything about it ... did he miss it? I'm just asking ... I didn't say it was your fault ... no ... I can't keep it warm ... it'll be dry ... what ... but it's his favorite ... well, what am I supposed to feed them ... of course they're hungry ... you're already an hour late ... well, you could have called ... "

I don't know how long my mom was on the phone because I couldn't stay at the table and listen. I went into my room and read. I wasn't hungry anymore anyway. I just wanted to be in a quiet place. After a little while, my mom came into the room. She said that dad had just called again, and they should be home in thirty minutes. She asked me if anything was wrong, and I knew that she didn't mean my sister, and I knew that she didn't mean she and Dad fighting on the phone because that stuff just happens sometimes. She just noticed that I looked very sad today, and she didn't think it was my friends leaving because I looked okay yesterday when I came back from sledding.

"Is it your aunt Helen?"

It was the way she said it that started me feeling.

"Please, don't do this to yourself, Charlie."

But I did do it to myself. Like I do every year on my birthday.

"I'm sorry."

My mom wouldn't let me talk about it. She knows that I stop listening and start to really breathe fast. She covered my mouth and wiped at my eyes. I calmed down enough to make it downstairs. And I calmed down enough to be glad when my brother came home. And when we ate dinner, it wasn't too dry. Then, we went outside to put up luminaria, which is an activity where all our neighbors fill brown paper bags with sand and line the street with them. Then, we stick a candle in the sand of each bag, and when we light the candles, it turns the street into a "landing strip" for Santa Claus. I love putting luminaria up every year because it is very beautiful and a tradition and a good distraction from my birthday.

My family gave me some really nice birthday presents. My sister was still mad at me, but she got me a Smiths record anyway. And my brother got me a poster signed by the whole football team. My dad gave me some records that my sister told him to buy. And my mom gave me some of the books she loved when she was a kid. One of them was *The Catcher in the Rye.*

I started reading my mom's copy from the place I left off with Bill's copy. And it made me not think about my birthday. All I thought was that I am going to take my driver's test sometime soon enough. That was a pretty good thing to think about. And then I thought about my driver's education class this past semester.

Mr. Smith, who is kind of short and smells funny, wouldn't let any of us turn on the radio as we rode around. There were also two sophomores, one boy and one girl. They used to secretly touch each other's legs in the backseat when it was my turn. Then, there was me. I wish I had a lot of stories about driver's education class. Sure, there were these movies about death on the highway. And sure there were police officers coming to talk to us. And sure it was fun to get my learner's permit, but Mom and Dad said they didn't want me driving until I absolutely had to because insurance is so expensive. And I could never ask Sam to drive her pickup truck. I just couldn't.

These kind of things kept me calm the night of my birthday.

The next morning Christmas started out nice. Dad liked his copy of *M*A*S*H* a lot, which made me so happy, especially when he told his own story about that night we watched it. He left out the part about him crying, but he winked at me, so I knew he remembered. Even the two-hour drive to Ohio was actually okay for the first half hour, even though I had to sit on the hump in the backseat, because my dad kept asking questions about college, and my brother kept talking. He is dating one of those cheerleader girls who does flips during college football games. Her name is Kelly. My dad was very interested in that. My sister made some remark about how cheerleading is stupid and sexist, and my brother told her to shut up. Kelly was majoring in philosophy. I asked my brother if Kelly was unconventionally beautiful.

"No, she's hot beautiful."

And my sister started talking about how the way a woman looks is not the most important thing. I agreed, but then my brother started saying how my sister was just a "bitchy dyke." Then, my mom told my brother to not use such language in front of me, which was strange considering I am probably the only one in the family with a friend

▷ **59** *wink at sb.:* jdm. zuzwinkern **61** *hump:* large lump that sticks out **63** *flip* (n): Salto, Flick-Flack **67** *major in sth.:* (cf. p. 182) **72** *bitchy dyke* (derog sl): aggressive lesbian

who is gay. Maybe not, but one who actually talks about it. I'm not sure. Regardless, my dad asked how my brother and Kelly met.

My brother and Kelly met at a restaurant called Ye Olde College Inn or something like that at Penn State. They supposedly have this famous dessert called "grilled stickies." Anyway, Kelly was with her sorority sisters, and they started to leave, and she dropped her book right in front of my brother, and she kept walking. My brother said that although Kelly denies this, he's sure that she dropped the book on purpose. The leaves were in full bloom when he caught up with her in front of the video arcade. That's how he described it anyway. They spent the rest of the afternoon playing old video games like Donkey Kong and feeling nostalgic, which as a general statement, I found sad and sweet. I asked my brother if Kelly drank cocoa.

"Are you high?"

And again my mom asked my brother not to use such language in front of me, which was strange again because I think I'm the only person in my family who's ever been high. Maybe also my brother. I'm not sure. Definitely not my sister. Then again, maybe my whole family has been high, and we just don't tell each other these things.

My sister spent the next ten minutes denouncing the Greek system of sororities and fraternities. She kept telling stories of "hazing" and how kids have died before. She then told this one story about how she heard there was a sorority that made the new girls stand in their underwear while they circled their "fat" in red magic markers. My brother had had enough of my sister at that point.

"Bullshit!"

I still can't believe that my brother swore in the car, and my dad or mom didn't say anything. I guess because he's in college now, it's all right. My sister didn't care about the word. She just kept going.

"It's not bullshit. I heard it."

"Watch your mouth, young lady," my dad said from the front seat.

"Oh, yeah? Where did you hear it?" my brother asked.

"I heard it on National Public Radio," my sister said.

"Oh, Jesus." My brother has a very full laugh.

"Well, I did."

My mom and dad looked like they were watching a tennis match through the windshield because they just kept shaking their heads. They didn't say anything. They didn't look back. I should point out, though, that my dad slowly started turning the Christmas music on the radio to a deafening volume.

"You are so full of shit. How would you know anything anyway? You haven't been to college. Kelly didn't go through anything like that."

"Oh, yeah ... like she'd tell you."

"Yeah ... she would. We don't keep secrets."

"Oh, you're such a sensitive new age guy."

I wanted them to stop fighting because I was starting to get upset, so I asked another question.

"Do you talk about books and issues?"

"Thank you for asking, Charlie. Yes. As a matter of fact we do. Kelly's favorite book just happens to be *Walden* by Henry David Thoreau. And Kelly just happened to say that the transcendental movement is a close parallel to this day and age."

"Oooo. Big words." My sister rolls her eyes better than anyone.

"Oh, I'm sorry. Was anyone talking to you? I happen to be telling my younger brother about my girlfriend. Kelly says that she hopes a good Democratic candidate will challenge George Bush. Kelly says that her hope is that the E.R.A. might finally pass if that happens. That's right. The E.R.A. that you always squawk about. Even cheerleaders think about those things. And they can actually have fun in the meantime."

My sister folded her arms in front of her and started whistling. My brother was too much on a roll to stop, though. I noticed that my dad's neck was getting very red.

"But there's another difference between you and her. You see ... Kelly believes in women's rights so much that she would never let a guy hit her. I guess I can't say that about you."

▷ **6** *sorority* (cf. p. 183) • *drop sth.:* let sth. fall **8** *deny sth.:* say sth. is not true **20** *denounce sth.:* strongly criticize sth. **21** *hazing* (AE): (cf. p. 182) **46** *new age guy:* (here) understanding and caring man **52–53** *transcendental movement:* (in the USA) mid-19th-century movement which believed that nature was a source of spiritual enlightenment; *Walden* (1854) is one of the main books expressing transcendental thought **57** *George Bush:* George Bush Sr., president of the USA (1989–1993) **58** *E.R.A.* (abbr) = *Equal Rights Amendment:* Zusatz zur US-amerikanischen Verfassung, der die Gleichberechtigung von Mann und Frau garantieren soll **59** *squawk* (v): speak in a loud sharp voice **63** *be on a roll* (infml): be feeling successful at what you are doing

I swear to God, we almost died. My dad hit those brakes so hard that my brother almost flew over the seat. When the smell from the tires started to fade, my dad took a deep breath and turned around. First, he turned to my brother. He didn't say a word. He just stared.

My brother looked at my dad like a deer caught by my cousins. After a long two seconds, my brother turned to my sister. I think he felt bad about it because of how the words came out.

"I'm sorry. Okay? I mean it. C'mon. Stop crying."

My sister was crying so hard, it was scary. Then, my dad turned to my sister. Again, he didn't say a word. He just snapped his fingers to distract her from crying. She looked at him. She was confused at first because he wasn't giving her a warm look. But then, she looked down and shrugged and turned to my brother.

"I'm sorry I said what I said about Kelly. She sounds nice."

Then, my dad turned to my mom. And my mom turned to us.

"Your father and I don't want any more fighting. Especially in the family's house. Understood?"

My mom and dad make a real team sometimes. It's amazing to watch. My brother and sister both nodded and looked down. Then, my dad turned to me.

"Charlie?"

"Yes, sir?"

It is important to say "sir" at these moments. And if they ever call you by your first-middle-last name, you better watch out. I'm telling you.

"Charlie, I would like you to drive the rest of the way to my mother's house."

Everyone in the car knew that this was probably the worst idea my dad ever had in his whole life. But no one argued. He got out of the car in the middle of the road. He got in the backseat between my brother and sister. I climbed in the front seat, stalled the car twice, and put on my seat belt. I drove the rest of the way. I haven't sweat that much since I played sports, and it was cold out.

My dad's family is kind of like my mom's family. My brother once said it was like the same cousins with different names. The big difference is my grandma. I love my grandma. Everyone loves my grandma. She was waiting for us in the driveway as she always did. She always knew when someone was coming.

"Is Charlie driving now?"

"He turned sixteen yesterday."

"Oh."

My grandma is very old, and she doesn't remember things a lot, but she bakes the most delicious cookies. When I was very little, we had my mom's mom, who always had candy, and my dad's mom, who always had cookies. My mom told me that when I was little, I called them "Candy Grandma" and "Cookies Grandma." I also called pizza crust "pizza bones." I don't know why I'm telling you this.

It's like my very first memory, which I guess is the first time I was aware that I was alive. My mom and my Aunt Helen took me to the zoo. I think I was three. I don't remember that part. Anyway, we were watching these two cows. A mother cow and its baby calf. And they didn't have a lot of room to walk around. Anyway, the baby calf was standing right underneath its mother, just kind of walking around, and the mother cow took a "dump" on the baby calf's head. I thought it was the funniest thing I had ever seen in the whole world, and I laughed about it for three hours. At first, my mom and Aunt Helen kind of laughed, too, because they were happy that I was laughing. Supposedly, I didn't talk hardly at all when I was a little kid, and whenever I seemed normal, they were happy. But into the third hour, they were trying to make me stop laughing, but it only made me laugh harder. I don't think it was really three hours, but it seemed like a long time. I still think about it every now and then. It seems like a rather "auspicious" beginning.

After hugs and handshakes, we went into my grandma's house, and the whole dad-side-of-the-family was there. Great Uncle Phil with his fake teeth and my aunt Rebecca, who is my dad's sister. Mom told us that Aunt Rebecca just got divorced again, so we shouldn't mention anything. All I could think about was the cookies, but Grandma didn't make them this year because of her bad hip.

We all sat down and watched television instead, and my cousins and my brother talked about football. And my Great Uncle Phil drank. And we ate dinner. And I had to sit at the little kids' table because there are more cousins on my dad's side of the family.

Little kids talk about the strangest things. They really do.

▷ **5** *deer:* Reh **31** *stall the car:* den Motor abwürgen **54** *take a "dump":* (here) shit **63** *auspicious* [ɔːˈspɪʃəs]: full of promise

After dinner is when we watched *It's a Wonderful Life*, and I started feeling more and more sad. As I was walking up the stairs to my dad's old room, and I was looking at the old photographs, I started thinking that there was a time when these weren't memories. That someone actually took that photograph, and the people in the photograph had just eaten lunch or something.

My grandma's first husband died in Korea. My dad and my aunt Rebecca were very young. And my grandma moved with her two kids to live with her brother, my great uncle Phil.

Finally, after a few years, my grandma was feeling very sad because she had these two little kids, and she was tired from waitressing all the time. So, one day, she was working at this diner where she worked, and this truck driver asked her on a date. My grandma was very very pretty in that old photograph kind of way. They dated for a while. And finally they got married. He turned out to be a terrible person. He hit my dad all the time. And he hit my aunt Rebecca all the time. And he really hit my grandma. All the time. And my grandma really couldn't do anything about it, I guess, because it went on for seven years.

It ended finally when my great uncle Phil saw bruises on my aunt Rebecca and finally got the truth out of my grandma. Then, he got a few of his friends together from the factory. And they found my grandma's second husband in a bar. And they beat him up really bad. My great uncle Phil loves to tell the story when my grandma isn't around. The story keeps changing, but the main point is still the same. The guy died four days later in the hospital.

I still don't know how my great uncle Phil missed going to jail for doing what he did. I asked my dad once, and he said that the people that lived around his neighborhood understood that some things had nothing to do with the police. He said that if someone touched your sister or your mother, they paid the price, and everyone looked the other way.

It's just too bad that it went on for seven years because my aunt Rebecca went through the same kind of husbands. My aunt Rebecca had it different, though, because neighborhoods change. My great uncle Phil was too old, and my dad left his hometown. She had to get restraining orders instead.

I think about what my three cousins, who are Aunt Rebecca's children, will turn out like. One girl and two boys. I get sad, too, because I think that the one girl will probably end up like my aunt

Rebecca, and the one boy will probably end up like his dad. The other boy might end up like my dad because he can really play sports, and he had a different dad than his brother or sister. My dad talks to him a lot and teaches him how to throw and hit a baseball. I used to get jealous about this when I was a little kid, but I don't anymore. Because my brother said that my cousin is the only one in his family who has a chance. He needs my dad. I guess I understand that now.

My dad's old room is very much the way he left it, except more faded. There is a globe on a desk that has been spun a lot. And there are old posters of baseball players. And old press clippings of my dad winning the big game when he was a sophomore. I don't know why, but I really understood why my dad had to leave this house. When he knew my grandma would never find another man because she was through trusting and would never look for anything else because she didn't know how. And when he saw his sister start bringing home younger versions of their stepfather to date. He just couldn't stay.

I laid down on his old bed, and I looked through the window at this tree that was probably a lot shorter when my dad looked at it. And I could feel what he felt on the night when he realized that if he didn't leave, it would never be his life. It would be theirs. At least that's how he's put it. Maybe that's why my dad's side of the family watches the same movie every year. It makes sense enough. I should probably mention that my dad never cries at the ending.

I don't know if my grandma or Aunt Rebecca will ever really forgive my dad for leaving them. Only my great uncle Phil understood that part. It's always strange to see how my dad changes around his mom and sister. He feels bad all the time, and his sister and he always take a walk alone together. One time, I looked out the window, and I saw my dad giving her money.

▷ **12** *diner* (AE): small, usu. cheap restaurant **19** *bruise* [bru:z]: blauer Fleck **36** *restraining order* (AE): official order stating that a husband is not allowed to see his family **49** *faded:* verblasst • *spin sth. – spun – spun:* turn sth. round and round **54** *be through doing sth.:* no longer be able to do sth.

I wonder what my aunt Rebecca says in the car on the way home. I wonder what her children think. I wonder if they talk about us. I wonder if they look at my family and wonder who has a chance to make it. I bet they do.

Love always,
Charlie

December 26, 1991

Dear friend,

I am sitting in my bedroom now after the two-hour ride back to my house. My sister and brother were nice to each other, so I didn't have to drive.

Usually, on the way home, we drive to visit my Aunt Helen's grave. It's kind of a tradition. My brother and my dad never want to go that much, but they know not to say anything because of Mom and me. My sister is kind of neutral, but she is sensitive about certain things.

Every time we go to see my Aunt Helen's grave, my mom and I like to talk about something really great about her. Most years it is about how she let me stay up and watch *Saturday Night Live.* And my mom smiles because she knows if she was a kid, she would have wanted to stay up and watch, too.

We both put down flowers and sometimes a card. We just want her to know that we miss her, and we think of her, and she was special. She didn't get that enough when she was alive, my mom always says. And like my dad, I think my mom feels guilty about it. So guilty that instead of giving her money, she gave her a home to stay in.

I want you to know why my mom is guilty. I should probably tell you why, but I really don't know if I should. I have to talk about it with someone. No one in my family will ever talk about it. It's just something they don't. I'm talking about the bad thing that happened to Aunt Helen they wouldn't tell me about when I was little.

Every time it comes to Christmas it's all I can think about … deep down. It is the one thing that makes me deep down sad.

I will not say who. I will not say when. I will just say that my aunt Helen was molested. I hate that word. It was done by someone who was very close to her. It was not her dad. She finally told her dad. He didn't believe her because of who it was. A friend of the family. That just made it worse. My grandma never said anything either. And the man kept coming over for visits.

My aunt Helen drank a lot. My aunt Helen took drugs a lot. My aunt Helen had many problems with men and boys. She was a very unhappy person most of her life. She went to hospitals all the time. All kinds of hospitals. Finally, she went to a hospital that helped her figure things out enough to try and make things normal, so she moved in with my family. She started taking classes to get a good job. She told her last bad man to leave her alone. She started losing weight without going on a diet. She took care of us, so my parents could go out and drink and play board games. She let us stay up late. She was the only person other than my mom and dad and brother and sister to buy me two presents. One for my birthday. One for Christmas. Even when she moved in with the family and had no money. She always bought me two presents. They were always the best presents.

On December 24, 1983, a policeman came to the door. My aunt Helen was in a terrible car accident. It was very snowy. The policeman told my mom that my aunt Helen had passed away. He was a very nice man because when my mom started crying, he said that it was a very bad accident, and my Aunt Helen was definitely killed instantly. In other words, there was no pain. There was no pain anymore.

The policeman asked my mom to come down and identify the body. My dad was still at work. That was when I walked up with my brother and sister. It was my seventh birthday. We all wore party hats. My mom made my sister and brother wear them. My sister saw Mom crying and asked what was wrong. My mom couldn't say anything. The policeman got on one knee and told us what happened. My brother and sister cried. But I didn't. I knew that the policeman made a mistake.

My mom asked my brother and sister to take care of me and left with the policeman. I think we watched TV. I don't think I really remember. My dad came home before my mom.

▷ **34** *molest sb.:* touch sb. (esp. a child or young person) sexually

"Why the long faces?"

We told him. He did not cry. He asked if we were okay. My brother and sister said no. I said yes. The policeman just made a mistake. It is very snowy. He probably couldn't see. My mom came home. She was crying. She looked at my dad and nodded. My dad held her. That's when I figured out that the policeman didn't make a mistake.

I don't really know what happened next, and I never really asked. I just remember going to the hospital. I remember sitting in a room with bright lights. I remember a doctor asking me questions. I remember telling him how Aunt Helen was the only one who hugged me. I remember seeing my family on Christmas day in a waiting room. I remember not being allowed to go to the funeral. I remember never saying good-bye to my Aunt Helen.

I don't know how long I kept going to the doctor. I don't remember how long they kept me out of school. It was a long time. I know that much. All I remember is the day I started getting better because I remembered the last thing my Aunt Helen said just before she left to drive in the snow.

She wrapped herself in a coat. I handed her the car keys because I was always the one who could find them. I asked Aunt Helen where she was going. She told me that it was a secret. I kept bugging my aunt Helen, which she loved. She loved the way I would keep asking her questions. She finally shook her head, smiled, and whispered in my ear.

"I'm going to buy your birthday present."

That's the last time I ever saw her. I like to think my aunt Helen would now have that good job she was studying for. I like to think she would have met a good man. I like to think she would have lost the weight she always wanted to lose without dieting.

Despite everything my mom and doctor and dad have said to me about blame, I can't stop thinking what I know. And I know that my aunt Helen would still be alive today if she just bought me one present like everybody else. She would be alive if I were born on a day that didn't snow. I would do anything to make this go away. I miss her terribly. I have to stop writing now because I am too sad.

Love always,
Charlie

December 30, 1991

Dear friend,

The day after I wrote to you, I finished *The Catcher in the Rye.* I have read it three times since. I really didn't know what else to do. Sam and Patrick are finally coming home tonight, but I won't get to see them. Patrick is going to meet Brad somewhere. Sam is going to meet Craig. I'll see them both tomorrow at the Big Boy and then at Bob's New Year's Eve party.

The exciting part is that I'm going to drive to the Big Boy by myself. My dad said I couldn't drive until the weather cleared up, and it finally did a little bit yesterday. I made a mix tape for the occasion. It is called "The First Time I Drove." Maybe I'm being too sentimental, but I like to think that when I'm old, I will be able to look at all these tapes and remember those drives.

The first time I drove alone was to see my aunt Helen. It was the first time I ever went to see her without at least my mom. I made it a special time. I bought flowers with my Christmas money. I even made her a mix tape and left it at the grave. I hope you do not think that makes me weird.

I told my aunt Helen all about my life. About Sam and Patrick. About their friends. About my first New Year's Eve party tomorrow. I told her about how my brother would be playing his last football game of the season on New Year's Day. I told her about my brother leaving and how my mom cried. I told her about the books I read. I told her about the song "Asleep." I told her when we all felt infinite. I told her about me getting my driver's license. How my mom drove us there. And how I drove us back. And how the policeman who ran the test didn't even look weird or have a funny name, which felt like a gyp to me.

I remember when I was just about to say good-bye to my aunt Helen, I started crying. It was a real kind of crying, too. Not the panicky type, which I do a lot. And I made Aunt Helen a promise to only cry about important things because I would hate to think that crying as much as I do would make crying for Aunt Helen less than it is.

▷ **10** *hug sb.:* jdn. umarmen **19** *wrap yourself in sth.:* sich in etwas einwickeln **21** *bug sb.* (infml): annoy or irritate sb. **66** *gyp* [dʒɪp] (AE infml): Betrug

Then, I said good-bye, and I drove home.

I read the book again that night because I knew that if I didn't, I would probably start crying again. The panicky type, I mean. I read until I was completely exhausted and had to go to sleep. In the morning, I finished the book and then started immediately reading it again. Anything to not feel like crying. Because I made the promise to Aunt Helen. And because I don't want to start thinking again. Not like I have this last week. I can't think again. Not ever again.

I don't know if you've ever felt like that. That you wanted to sleep for a thousand years. Or just not exist. Or just not be aware that you do exist. Or something like that. I think wanting that is very morbid, but I want it when I get like this. That's why I'm trying not to think. I just want it all to stop spinning. If this gets any worse, I might have to go back to the doctor. It's getting that bad again.

Love always,
Charlie

January 1, 1992

Dear friend,

It's now 4 o'clock in the morning, which is the new year even though it's still December 31, that is, until people sleep. I can't sleep. Everyone else is either asleep or having sex. I've been watching cable television and eating jello. And seeing things move. I wanted to tell you about Sam and Patrick and Craig and Brad and Bob and everyone, but I can't remember right now.

It's peaceful outside. I do know that. And I drove to the Big Boy earlier. And I saw Sam and Patrick. And they were with Brad and Craig. And it made me very sad because I wanted to be alone with them. This has never come up before.

Things were worse an hour ago, and I was looking at this tree but it was a dragon and then a tree, and I remembered that one nice pretty weather day when I was part of the air. And I remembered that I mowed the lawn that day for my allowance just like I shovel the driveway for my allowance now. So I started shoveling Bob's driveway, which is a strange thing to do at a New Year's Eve party really.

My cheeks were red cold just like Mr. Z's drinking face and his black shoes and his voice saying when a caterpillar goes into a cocoon, it goes through torture and how it takes seven years to digest gum. And this one kid Mark at the party who gave me this came out of nowhere and looked at the sky and told me to see the stars. So, I looked up, and we were in this giant dome like a glass snowball, and Mark said that the amazing white stars were really only holes in the black glass of the dome, and when you went to heaven, the glass broke away, and there was nothing but a whole sheet of star white, which is brighter than anything but doesn't hurt your eyes. It was vast and open and thinly quiet, and I felt so small.

Sometimes, I look outside, and I think that a lot of other people have seen this snow before. Just like I think that a lot of other people have read those books before. And listened to those songs.

I wonder how they feel tonight.

I don't really know what I'm saying. I probably shouldn't write this down because I'm still seeing things move. I want them to stop moving, but they're not supposed to for another few hours. That's what Bob said before he went to his bedroom with Jill, a girl that I don't know.

I guess what I'm saying is that this all feels very familiar. But it's not mine to be familiar about. I just know that another kid has felt this. This one time when it's peaceful outside, and you're seeing things move, and you don't want to, and everyone is asleep. And all the books you've read have been read by other people. And all the songs you've loved have been heard by other people. And that girl that's pretty to you is pretty to other people. And you know that if you looked at these facts when you were happy, you would feel great because you are describing "unity."

It's like when you are excited about a girl and you see a couple holding hands, and you feel so happy for them. And other times you see the same couple, and they make you so mad. And all you want is to always feel happy for them because you know that if you do, then it means that you're happy, too.

▷ **22** *jello* (BE: *jelly*): Wackelpudding **32** *shovel sth.* [ˌʃʌvl]: etwas freischaufeln **36** *caterpillar* [ˈkætərpɪlər]: Raupe **40** *dome:* round-roofed building **55** *familiar:* well known to you

I just remembered what made me think of all this. I'm going to write it down because maybe if I do I won't have to think about it. And I won't get upset. But the thing is that I can hear Sam and Craig having sex, and for the first time in my life, I understand the end of that poem.

And I never wanted to. You have to believe me.

Love always,
Charlie

part 3

January 4, 1992

Dear friend,

I'm sorry for that last letter. To tell you the truth, I don't really remember much of it, but I know from how I woke up that it probably wasn't very nice. All I remember from the rest of that night was looking all over the house for an envelope and a stamp. When I finally found them, I wrote your address and walked down the hill past the trees to the post office because I knew that if I didn't put it in a mailbox that I couldn't get it back from, I would never mail the letter.

It's weird how important it seemed at the time.

Once I got to the post office, I dropped the letter into the mailbox. And it felt final. And calm. Then, I started throwing up, and I didn't stop throwing up until the sun came up. I looked at the road and saw a lot of cars, and I knew they were all going to their grandparents' house. And I knew a lot of them would watch my brother play football later that day. And my mind played hopscotch.

My brother ... football ... Brad ... Dave and his girlfriend in my room ... the coats ... the cold ... the winter ... "Autumn Leaves" ... don't tell anyone ... you pervert ... Sam and Craig ... Sam ... Christmas ... typewriter ... gift ... Aunt Helen ... and the trees kept moving ... they just wouldn't stop moving ... so I laid down and made a snow angel.

The policemen found me pale blue and asleep.

I didn't stop shivering from the cold until a long time after my mom and dad drove me home from the emergency room. Nobody got in trouble because these things used to happen to me when I was a kid when I was seeing the doctors. I would just wander off and fall asleep somewhere. Everyone knew I went to a party, but nobody, not even my sister, thought it was because of that. And I kept my mouth shut because I didn't want Sam or Patrick or Bob or anyone to get in trouble. But most of all, I didn't want to see my mother's face and especially my father's if they heard me say the truth.

So, I didn't say anything.

I just kept quiet and looked around. And I noticed things. The dots on the ceiling. Or how the blanket they gave me was rough. Or how the doctor's face looked rubbery. Or how everything was a deafening whisper, when he said that maybe I should start seeing a psychiatrist again. It was the first time a doctor ever told that to my parents with me in the room. And his coat was so white. And I was so tired.

All I could think through the whole day was that we missed my brother's football game because of me, and I really hoped my sister thought to tape it.

Luckily, she did.

We got home, and my mom made me some tea, and my dad asked me if I wanted to sit and watch the game, and I said yes. We watched my brother make a great play, but this time, nobody really cheered. All corners of all eyes were on me. And my mom said a lot of encouraging things about how I was doing so well this school year and maybe the doctor would help me sort things out. My mom can be quiet and talk at the same time when she's being positive. My dad kept giving me "love pats." Love pats are soft punches of encouragement that are administered on the knee, shoulder, and arm. My sister said that she could help me fix up my hair. It was weird to have them pay so much attention to me.

"What do you mean? What's wrong with my hair?"

My sister just kind of looked around, uncomfortable. I reached my hands up to my hair and realized that a lot of it was gone. I honestly don't remember when I did it, but from the look of my hair, I must have grabbed a pair of scissors and just started cutting without strategy. Big chunks of it were missing all over the place. It was like a butcher's cut. I hadn't looked at myself in the mirror at the party for a long time because my face was different and frightened me. Or else I would have noticed.

My sister did help me trim it up a bit, and I was lucky because everyone in school including Sam and Patrick thought it looked cool.

"Chic" was Patrick's word.

Regardless, I decided to never take LSD again.

Love always,
Charlie

▷ **12** *throw up* (infml): sich übergeben **16** *hopscotch:* children's game in which you hop (on one foot) through a series of squares drawn on the ground **22** *snow angel:* image made in the snow when a person lies on his or her back and then moves his or her arms to make an imprint that looks like wings **37** *psychiatrist* [saɪ'kaɪətrɪst] **61** *butcher* [bʊtʃər]: Metzger/in

January 14, 1992

Dear friend,

I feel like a big faker because I've been putting my life back together, and nobody knows. It's hard to sit in my bedroom and read like I always did. It's even hard to talk to my brother on the phone. His team finished third in the nation. Nobody told him we missed the game live because of me.

I went to the library and checked out a book because I was getting scared. Every now and then things would start moving again, and sounds were bass heavy and hollow. And I couldn't put a thought together. The book said that sometimes people take LSD, and they don't really get out of it. They said that it increases this one type of brain transmitter. They said that essentially the drug is twelve hours of schizophrenia, and if you already have a lot of this brain transmitter, you don't get out of it.

I started breathing fast in the library. It was really bad because I remembered some of the schizophrenic kids in the hospital when I was little. And it didn't help that this was the day after I noticed that all the kids were wearing their new Christmas clothes, so I decided to wear my new suit from Patrick to school, and was teased mercilessly for nine straight hours. It was such a bad day. I skipped my first class ever and went to see Sam and Patrick outside.

"Looking sharp, Charlie," Patrick said grinning.

"Can I have a cigarette?" I said. I couldn't bring myself to say "bum a smoke." Not for my first one. I just couldn't.

"Sure," said Patrick.

Sam stopped him.

"What's wrong, Charlie?"

I told them what was wrong, which prompted Patrick to keep asking me if I had a "bad trip."

"No. No. It's not that." I was really getting upset.

Sam put her arm around my shoulder, and she said she knew what I was going through. She told me I shouldn't worry about it. Once you do it, you remember how things looked on it. That's all. Like how the road turned into waves. And how your face was plastic and your eyes were two different sizes. It's all in your mind.

That's when she gave me the cigarette.

When I lit it, I didn't cough. It actually felt soothing. I know that's bad in a health class way, but it was true.

"Now, focus on the smoke," Sam said.

And I focused on the smoke.

"Now, that looks normal doesn't it?"

"Uh-huh," I think I said.

"Now, look at the cement on the playground. Is it moving?"

"Uh-huh."

"Okay ... now focus on the piece of paper that's just sitting there on the ground."

And I focused on the piece of paper that was sitting on the ground.

"Is the cement moving now?"

"No. It's not."

From there you go, to you're going to be okay, to you probably should never do acid again, Sam went on to explain what she called "the trance." The trance happens when you don't focus on anything, and the whole big picture swallows and moves around you. She said it was usually metaphoric, but for people who should never do acid again, it was literal.

That's when I started laughing. I was so relieved. And Sam and Patrick smiled. I was glad they started smiling, too, because I couldn't stand their looking so worried.

Things have stopped moving for the most part ever since. I haven't skipped another class. And I guess now I don't feel like a big faker for trying to put my life back together. Bill thought my paper on *The Catcher in the Rye* (which I wrote on my new old typewriter!) was my best one yet. He said I was "developing" at a rapid pace and gave me a different kind of book as "a reward." It's *On the Road* by Jack Kerouac.

I'm now up to about ten cigarettes a day.

Love always,
Charlie

▷ **3** *faker:* person who pretends to be sth. which he or she is not **10** *bass* [beɪs]: deep-sounding **13** *brain transmitter:* substance (here, serotonin) in the brain that carries some kind of information **14** *schizophrenia* [ˌskɪtsəˈfriːniə]: mental illness that causes identity problems **21** *skip sth.:* (here) not attend sth. **21–22** *my first ... ever:* ... for the very first time **23** *sharp* (infml): fashionable **30** *bad trip:* bad experience due to drugs **52** *do acid* (infml): take LSD **55** *metaphoric:* (here): not happening in reality **56** *literal:* (here) real **65** *Jack Kerouac* (1922–1969): American author and part of the Beat Generation

January 25, 1992

Dear friend,

I feel great! I really mean it. I have to remember this for the next time I'm having a terrible week. Have you ever done that? You feel really bad, and then it goes away, and you don't know why. I try to remind myself when I feel great like this that there will be another terrible week coming someday, so I should store up as many great details as I can, so during the next terrible week, I can remember those details and believe that I'll feel great again. It doesn't work a lot, but I think it's very important to try.

My psychiatrist is a very nice man. He's much better than my last psychiatrist. We talk about things that I feel and think and remember. Like when I was little, and there was this one time that I walked down the street in my neighborhood. I was completely naked, holding a bright blue umbrella, even though it wasn't raining. And I was so happy because it made my mom smile. And she rarely smiled. So, she took a picture. And the neighbors complained.

This other time, I saw a commercial for this movie about a man who was accused of murder, but he didn't commit the murder. A guy from *M*A*S*H* was the star of the movie. That's probably why I remember it. The commercial said that the whole movie was about him trying to prove that he was innocent and how he could go to jail anyway. That scared me a lot. It scared me how much it scared me. Being punished for something you did not do. Or being an innocent victim. It's just something that I never want to experience.

I don't know if it is important to tell you all this, but at the time, it felt like a "breakthrough."

The best thing about my psychiatrist is that he has music magazines in his waiting room. I read an article about Nirvana on one visit, and it didn't have any references to honey mustard dressing or lettuce. They kept talking about the singer's stomach problems all the time, though. It was weird.

Like I told you, Sam and Patrick love their big song, so I thought I'd read it to have something to discuss with them. In the end, the magazine compared him with John Lennon from the Beatles. I told that to Sam later, and she got really mad. She said he was like Jim Morrison if he was like anybody, but really, he isn't like anybody but himself. We were all at the Big Boy after *Rocky Horror*, and it started this big discussion.

Craig said the problem with things is that everyone is always comparing everyone with everyone and because of that, it discredits people, like in his photography classes.

Bob said that it was all about our parents not wanting to let go of their youth and how it kills them when they can't relate to something.

Patrick said that the problem was that since everything has happened already, it makes it hard to break new ground. Nobody can be as big as the Beatles because the Beatles already gave it a "context." The reason they were so big is that they had no one to compare themselves with, so the sky was the limit.

Sam added that nowadays a band or someone would compare themselves to the Beatles after the second album, and their own personal voice would be less from that moment on.

"What do you think, Charlie?"

I couldn't remember where I heard it or read it. I said maybe it was in *This Side of Paradise* by F. Scott Fitzgerald. There's a place near the end of the book where the main kid is picked up by some older gentleman. They are both going to an Ivy League homecoming football game, and they have this debate. The older gentleman is established. The kid is "jaded."

Anyway, they have this discussion, and the kid is an idealist in a temporary way. He talks about his "restless generation" and things like that. And he says something like, "This is not a time for heroes because nobody will let that happen." The book takes place in the 1920s, which I thought was great because I supposed the same kind of conversation could happen in the Big Boy. It probably already did with our parents and grandparents. It was probably happening with us right now.

So, I said I thought the magazine was trying to make him a hero, but then later somebody might dig up something to make him seem

▷ **36–37** *Jim Morrison* (1943–1971): American singer-songwriter of the band The Doors **41** *discredit sb.*: make sb. seem to have less worth than he or she has **57** *Ivy League* ['aɪvi ˌliːg]: a group of eight universities in the North East of the USA which have a high social and academic status **59** *established:* (here) settled with a good job, a family, etc. • *jaded* ['dʒeɪdəd]: tired and bored because you have seen too much of life

like less than a person. And I didn't know why because to me he is just a guy who writes songs that a lot of people like, and I thought that was enough for everyone involved. Maybe I'm wrong, but everyone at the table starting talking about it.

Sam blamed television. Patrick blamed government. Craig blamed the "corporate media." Bob was in the bathroom.

I don't know what it was, and I know we didn't really accomplish anything, but it felt great to sit there and talk about our place in things. It was like when Bill told me to "participate." I went to the homecoming dance like I told you before, but this was much more fun. It was especially fun to think that people all over the world were having similar conversations in their equivalent of the Big Boy.

I would have told the table that, but they were really having fun being cynical, and I didn't want to ruin it. So, I just sat back a little bit and watched Sam sitting next to Craig and tried not to be too sad about it. I have to say that I couldn't do it very successfully. But at one point, Craig was talking about something, and Sam turned to me and smiled. It was a movie smile in slow motion, and then everything was okay.

I told this to my psychiatrist, but he said it was too soon to draw any conclusions.

I don't know. I just had a great day. I hope you did, too.

Love always,
Charlie

February 2, 1992

Dear friend,

On the Road was a very good book. Bill didn't ask me to write a paper about it because, like I said, it was "a reward." He did ask me to visit him in his office after school to discuss it, which I did. He made tea, and I felt like a grown-up. He even let me smoke a cigarette in his office, but he urged me to quit smoking because of the health risks. He even had a pamphlet in his desk that he gave me. I now use it as a bookmark.

I thought Bill and I were going to talk about the book, but we ended up talking about "things." It was great to have so many discussions back-to-back. Bill asked me about Sam and Patrick and my parents, and I told him about getting my license and talking in the Big Boy. I also told him about my psychiatrist. I didn't tell him about the party or my sister and her boyfriend, though. They're still seeing each other in secret, which my sister says only "adds to their passion."

After I got through telling Bill about my life, I asked him about his. It was nice, too, because he didn't try to be cool and relate to me or anything. He was just himself about it. He said that he studied undergraduate work at some college in the West that doesn't give grades, which I thought was peculiar, but Bill said it was the best education he ever got. He said he'd give me a brochure when the time was right.

After he went to Brown University for graduate school, Bill traveled around Europe for a while, and when he came home, he joined Teach for America. When this year is over, he thinks he is going to move to New York and write plays. I guess he's still pretty young, although I thought it would be rude to ask him. I did ask him if he had a girlfriend, though, and he said he didn't. He seemed sad when he said it, too, but I decided not to pry because I thought that would be too personal. Then, he gave me my next book to read. It's called *Naked Lunch*.

I started reading it when I got home, and to tell you the truth, I don't know what the guy is talking about. I would never tell Bill this. Sam told me that William S. Burroughs wrote the book when he was on heroin and that I should "go with the flow." So, I did. I still had no idea what he was talking about, so I went downstairs to watch television with my sister.

The show was *Gomer Pyle*, and my sister was very quiet and moody. I tried to talk to her, but she just told me to shut up and leave

▷ **7** *accomplish sth.* [ə'kɑːmplɪʃ; BE ə'kʌm-]: be successful in sth. **12** *equivalent of sth.*: thing that serves the same purpose as sth. **14** *cynical:* very critical **36** *back-to-back* (AE infml): one right after the other **43–44** *undergraduate work:* (cf p. 183) **47** *graduate school:* (cf. p. 182) **49** *Teach for America:* organization that recruits college graduates to teach in poor public schools for two years in order to give an equal chance in life for all American school children **53** *pry:* ask personal questions about sb. **55** *"Naked Lunch":* novel (1959) by William S. Burroughs (1914–1997) **59** *go with the flow* (infml): let yourself be guided by the feelings sth. evokes **62** *"Gomer Pyle":* 1960s TV series about a stupid but nice recruit in the army

her alone. So, I watched the show for a few minutes, but it made even less sense to me than the book, so I decided to do my math homework, which was a mistake because math has never made any sense to me.

I was just confused all day.

So, I tried to help my mother in the kitchen, but I dropped the casserole, so she told me to read in my room until my father came home, but reading is what started this whole mess in the first place. Luckily, my father came home before I could pick up the book again, but he told me to stop "hanging on his shoulders like a monkey" because he wanted to watch the hockey game. I watched the hockey game with him for a while, but I couldn't stop asking him questions about which countries the players are from, and he was "resting his eyes," which means he was sleeping but didn't want me to change the channel. So, he told me to go watch television with my sister, which I did, but she told me to go help my mother in the kitchen, which I did, but then she told me to go read in my room. Which I did.

I've read about a third of the book now, and it's pretty good so far.

Love always,
Charlie

February 8, 1992

Dear friend,

I have a date for the Sadie Hawkins' dance. In case you didn't have one of those, it's the dance where the girl asks the boy. In my case, the girl is Mary Elizabeth, and the boy is me. Can you believe it?!

I think it started when I was helping Mary Elizabeth staple the latest issue of *Punk Rocky* on Friday before we went to *The Rocky Horror Picture Show*. Mary Elizabeth was so nice that day. She said that it was the best issue we'd ever had for two reasons, and both of those reasons were mine.

First of all, it was in color, and second, it had the poem that I gave Patrick in it.

It really was a great issue. I think I'll even think so when I'm older. Craig included some of his color photographs. Sam included some "underground" news on some bands. Mary Elizabeth wrote an article about the Democratic candidates. Bob included a reprint of a pro-hemp pamphlet. And Patrick made this fake coupon advertising a free "blow job" for anyone who buys a Smiley Cookie at the Big Boy. *Some restrictions apply!*

There was even a nude photograph (from the back) of Patrick if you can believe it. Sam had Craig take the picture. Mary Elizabeth told everyone to keep it a secret that the photograph was Patrick, which everybody did, except Patrick.

All night, he kept yelling, "Flaunt it, baby! Flaunt it!" which is his favorite line from his favorite movie, *The Producers.*

Mary Elizabeth told me she thought that Patrick asked her to put the photograph in the issue so Brad could have a photograph of him without it being suspicious, but he wouldn't say for sure. Brad bought a copy without even looking at it, so maybe she was right.

When I went to *The Rocky Horror Picture Show* that night, Mary Elizabeth was really mad because Craig didn't show up. Nobody knew why. Not even Sam. The problem was nobody was there to play Rocky, the muscular robot (I'm not quite sure what he is). After looking around at everybody, Mary Elizabeth turned to me.

"Charlie, how many times have you seen the show?"

"Ten."

"Do you think you can play Rocky?"

"I'm not cut and hunky."

"It doesn't matter. Can you play him?"

"I guess."

"Do you guess or do you know?"

"I guess."

"Good enough."

The next thing I know, I was wearing nothing but slippers and a bathing suit, which somebody painted gold. I don't know how these things happen to me sometimes. I was very nervous, especially because in the show, Rocky has to touch Janet all over her body, and

▷ **7** *casserole:* dish in which a stew (= *Eintopf*) is cooked in an oven **26** *staple sth.:* etwas zusammenheften **36–37** *pro-hemp:* in favour of marijuana **39** *Some restrictions apply!:* There are some limits to this offer **44** *flaunt sth.:* show sth. openly to impress people **45** *"The Producers":* musical comedy (1968) directed by Mel Brooks (born 1928)

Sam was playing Janet. Patrick kept making jokes that I would get an "erection." I really hoped this wouldn't happen. Once, I got an erection in class and had to go to the blackboard. It was a terrible time. And when my mind took that experience and added a spotlight and the fact that I was only wearing a bathing suit, I panicked. I almost didn't do the show, but then Sam told me she really wanted me to play Rocky, and I guess that's all I really needed to hear.

I won't go into detail about the whole show, but I had the best time I ever had in my whole life. I'm not kidding. I got to pretend that I was singing, and I got to dance around, and I got to wear a "feather boa" in the grande finale, which I wouldn't have thought anything of because it's part of the show, but Patrick couldn't stop talking about it.

"Charlie in a feather boa! Charlie in a feather boa!" He just couldn't stop laughing.

But the best part was the scene with Janet where we had to touch each other. It wasn't the best part because I got to touch Sam and have her touch me. It's the exact opposite. I know that sounds dumb, but it's true. Just before the scene, I thought about Sam, and I thought that if I touched her in that way on stage and meant it, it would be cheap. And as much as I think I might want to someday touch her like that, I never want it to be cheap. I don't want it to be Rocky and Janet. I want it to be Sam and I. And I want her to mean it back. So, we just played.

When the show was over, we all bowed together, and there was applause everywhere. Patrick even shoved me in front of the rest of the cast to take my own personal bow. I think this is the initiation for new cast members. All I could think was how nice it was that everyone applauded for me and how glad I was that nobody in my family was there to see me play Rocky in a feather boa. Especially my dad.

I did get an erection, though, but not until later, in the parking lot of the Big Boy.

That's when Mary Elizabeth asked me to the Sadie Hawkins' dance after she said, "You looked really good in your costume."

I like girls. I really do. Because they can think you look good in a bathing suit even when you don't. The erection made me feel guilty in hindsight though, but I guess it couldn't be helped.

I told my sister about having a date for the dance, but she was really distracted. Then, I tried to ask her advice about how to treat a girl on a date since I've never had a date before, but she wouldn't answer. She wasn't being mean. She was just "staring off into space." I asked her if she was okay, and she said that she needed to be alone, so I went up and finished *Naked Lunch*.

After I finished, I just laid around in my bed, looking at the ceiling, and I smiled because it was a nice kind of quiet.

Love always,
Charlie

February 9, 1992

Dear friend,

I have to say something about my last letter. I know that Sam would never ask me to the dance. I know that she would bring Craig, and if not Craig, then Patrick since Brad's girlfriend, Nancy, is going with Brad. I think Mary Elizabeth is a really smart and pretty person, and I'm glad that she is my first date ever. But after I said yes, and Mary Elizabeth announced it to the group, I wanted Sam to be jealous. I know it's wrong to want something like that, but I really did.

Sam wasn't jealous, though. To tell you the truth, I don't think she could have been happier about it, which was hard.

She even told me how to treat a girl on a date, which was very interesting. She said that with a girl like Mary Elizabeth, you shouldn't tell her she looks pretty. You should tell her how nice her outfit is because her outfit is her choice whereas her face isn't. She also said that with some girls, you should do things like open car doors and buy flowers, but with Mary Elizabeth (especially since it's the Sadie Hawkins' dance), I shouldn't do that. So, I asked her what I should do, and she said that I should ask a lot of questions and not mind when Mary Elizabeth doesn't stop talking. I said that it didn't sound very democratic, but Sam said she does it all the time with boys.

▷ **10** *get to do sth.:* have the opportunity to do sth. • *feather boa:* a kind of long "scarf" made of feathers, worn across the shoulders (usu. by women) **36–37** *in hindsight* ['haɪndsaɪt]: looking back **37** *it can't be helped:* there is no way out of a situation

Sam did say that sex things were tricky with Mary Elizabeth since she's had boyfriends before and is a lot more experienced than I am. She said that the best thing to do when you don't know what to do during anything sexual is pay attention to how that person is kissing you and kiss them back the same way. She says that is very sensitive, which I certainly want to be.

So, I said, "Can you show me?"

And she said, "Don't be smart."

We talk to each other like that every now and then. It always makes her laugh. After Sam showed me a Zippo lighter trick, I asked her more about Mary Elizabeth.

"What if I don't want to do anything sexual with her?"

"Just say you're not ready."

"Does that work?"

"Sometimes."

I wanted to ask Sam about the other side of "sometimes," but I didn't want to be too personal, and I didn't want to know deep down. I wish I could stop being in love with Sam. I really do.

Love always,
Charlie

February 15, 1992

Dear friend,

I don't feel very well because everything is messy. I did go to the dance, and I did tell Mary Elizabeth how nice her outfit was. I did ask her questions, and I let her talk the whole time. I learned a lot about "objectification," Native Americans, and the bourgeoisie.

But most of all, I learned about Mary Elizabeth.

Mary Elizabeth wants to go to Berkeley and get two degrees. One is for political science. The other is for sociology with a minor concentration in women's studies. Mary Elizabeth hates high school and wants to explore lesbian relationships. I asked her if she thought girls were pretty, and she looked at me like I was stupid and said, "That's not the point."

Mary Elizabeth's favorite movie is *Reds*. Her favorite book is an autobiography of a woman who was a character in *Reds*. I can't remember her name. Mary Elizabeth's favorite color is green. Her favorite season is spring. Her favorite ice cream flavor (she said she refuses to eat low-fat frozen yogurt on principle alone) is Cherry Garcia. Her favorite food is pizza (half mushrooms, half green peppers). Mary Elizabeth is a vegetarian, and she hates her parents. She is also fluent in Spanish.

The only thing she asked me the whole time was whether or not I wanted to kiss her good night. When I said that I wasn't ready, she said she understood and told me what a great time she had. She said I was the most sensitive boy she'd ever met, which I didn't understand because really all I did was not interrupt her.

Then, she asked me if I wanted to go out again sometime, which Sam and I hadn't discussed, so I wasn't prepared to answer it. I said yes because I didn't want to do anything wrong, but I don't think I can think of a whole other night's worth of questions. I don't know what to do. How many dates can you go on and still not be ready to kiss? I don't think I will ever be ready for Mary Elizabeth. I'll have to ask Sam about this.

Incidentally, Sam took Patrick to the dance after Craig said he was too busy. I guess they had a big fight about it. Finally, Craig said that he didn't want to go to some stupid high school dance since he had already graduated. At one point in the dance, Patrick went to the parking lot to get stoned with his guidance counselor, and Mary Elizabeth was requesting that the deejay play some girl bands, which left Sam and me alone.

"Are you having a good time?"

Sam didn't answer right away. She just kind of looked sad.

"Not really. Are you?"

"I don't know. This is my first date, so I don't know what to compare it to."

"Don't worry. You'll do fine."

▷ **10** *Zippo:* company that produces lighters (= *Feuerzeuge*) **26** *objectification:* act of treating people as if they are (esp. sexual) objects with no feelings • *the bourgeoisie* [ˌbʊrʒwɑːˈzi; BE ˌbʊəʒ-]: the capitalistically-oriented middle classes **28** *Berkeley:* famous university in California **34** *"Reds":* US film (1981) about left-wing American journalists during the 1917 Russian Revolution

"Really?"

"You want some punch?"

"Sure."

With that, Sam left. She really did look sad, and I wished I could have made her feel better, but sometimes, I guess you just can't. So, I stood alone by the wall and watched the dance for a while. I would describe it to you, but I think it's the kind of thing where you have to be there or at least know the people. But then again, maybe you knew the same people when you went to your high school dances, if you know what I mean.

The one different thing about this particular dance was my sister. She was with her boyfriend. And during a slow song, it looked like they had a huge fight because he stopped looking at her, and she rushed off the dance floor to where the bathrooms are. I tried to follow her, but she had too much of a head start. She never came back to the dance, and her boyfriend eventually left.

After Mary Elizabeth dropped me off, I went into the house and found my sister crying in the basement. This was a different kind of crying. It kind of frightened me. I talked very quiet and slow.

"Are you okay?"

"Leave me alone, Charlie."

"No, really. What's wrong?"

"You wouldn't understand."

"I could try."

"That's a laugh. That's really a laugh."

"Do you want me to wake up Mom and Dad then?"

"No."

"Well, maybe they could—"

"CHARLIE! SHUT UP! OKAY?! JUST SHUT UP!"

That's when she really started crying. I didn't want to make her feel worse, so I turned to leave her alone. That's when my sister started hugging me. She didn't say anything. She just hugged me tight and wouldn't let go. So, I hugged her back. It was weird, too, because I've never hugged my sister. Not when she wasn't forced to anyway. After a while, she calmed down a bit and let go. She took a deep breath and brushed off the hair that was sticking to her face.

That's when she told me she was pregnant.

I would tell you about the rest of the night, but I honestly don't remember much about it. It's all a very sad daze. I do know that her boyfriend said it wasn't his baby, but my sister knew that it was. And I do know that he broke up with her right there at the dance. My sister hasn't told anybody else about it because she doesn't want it to get around. The only people who know are me, her, and him. I'm not allowed to tell anyone we know. Not anyone. Not ever.

I told my sister that after a while, she probably couldn't hide it, but she said she wouldn't let it go that far. Since she was eighteen, she didn't need Mom or Dad's permission. All she needed was someone to be with her next Saturday at the clinic. And that person was me.

"It's lucky I got my license now."

I said that to make her laugh. But she didn't.

Love always,
Charlie

February 23, 1992

Dear friend,

I was sitting in the waiting room of the clinic. I had been there for an hour or so. I don't remember exactly how long. Bill had given me a new book to read, but I just couldn't concentrate on it. I guess it makes sense why not.

Then, I tried to read some magazines, but again, I just couldn't. It wasn't so much that they mentioned what the people were eating. It was all the magazine covers. Each one had a smiling face, and every time it was a woman on the cover, she was showing her cleavage. I wondered if those women wanted to do that to look pretty or if it was just part of the job. I wondered if they had a choice or not if they wanted to be successful. I just couldn't get that thought out of my mind.

I could almost see the photo shoot and the actress or model going to eat a "light lunch" with her boyfriend afterward. I could see him

▷ **2** *punch:* Bowle **15** *have a head start:* (here) be already far ahead because you started moving before anyone else **17** *drop sb. off:* take sb. to a place by car and drive away when he or she has got out of the car **39** *daze* (n): state of confusion **62** *cleavage* ['kli:vɪdʒ]: the top part of a woman's bosom as revealed in a low-cut dress or blouse

asking her about her day, and how she wouldn't think too much of it, or maybe if it was her first magazine cover, how she would be very excited because she was starting to become famous. I could see the magazine on the newsstands, and a lot of anonymous eyes looking at it, and how some people would think it was very important. And then how a girl like Mary Elizabeth would be very angry about the actress or model showing her cleavage along with all the other actresses and models doing the same thing, while some photographer like Craig would just look at the quality of the photograph. Then, I thought there would be some men who would buy the magazine and masturbate to it. And I wondered what the actress or her boyfriend thought about that, if they did at all. And then I thought that it was about time for me to stop thinking because it wasn't doing my sister any good.

That's when I started thinking about my sister.

I thought about the time when she and her friends painted my fingernails, and how that was okay because my brother wasn't there. And the time she let me use her dolls to make up plays or let me watch whatever I wanted to watch on TV. And when she started becoming a "young lady," and no one was allowed to look at her because she thought she was fat. And how she really wasn't fat. And how she was actually very pretty. And how different her face looked when she realized boys thought she was pretty. And how different her face looked the first time she really liked a boy who was not on a poster on her wall. And how her face looked when she realized she was in love with that boy. And then I wondered how her face would look when she came out from behind those doors.

My sister was the one who told me where babies come from. My sister was also the one who laughed when I immediately asked her where babies go to.

When I thought that, I started to cry. But I couldn't let anyone see me because if they did, they might not let me drive her home, and they might call our parents. And I couldn't let that happen because my sister was counting on me, and this was the first time anyone ever counted on me for anything. When I realized that this was the first time I cried since I made my aunt Helen the promise not to cry unless it was for something important, I had to go outside because I couldn't hide it from anyone anymore.

I must have been in the car for a long time because eventually my sister found me there. I was chain-smoking cigarettes and crying still. My sister knocked on the window. I rolled it down. She looked at me with this curious expression. Then, her curiosity turned to anger.

"Charlie, are you smoking?!"

She was so mad. I can't tell you how mad she was.

"I can't believe you're smoking!"

That's when I stopped crying. And started laughing. Because of all the things she could have said right after she got out of there, she picked my smoking. And she got angry about it. And I knew if my sister was angry, then her face wouldn't be that different. And she would be okay.

"I'm going to tell Mom and Dad, you know?"

"No, you're not." God, I couldn't stop laughing.

When my sister thought about it for a second, I think she figured out why she wouldn't tell Mom or Dad. It's like she suddenly remembered where we were and what had just happened and how crazy our whole conversation was considering all that. Then, she started laughing.

But the laughing made her feel sick, so I had to get out of the car and help her into the backseat. I had already set up the pillow and blanket for her because we figured it was probably best for her to sleep it off a little in the car before we went home.

Just before she fell asleep, she said, "Well, if you're going to smoke, crack the window at least."

Which made me start laughing again.

"Charlie, smoking. I can't believe it."

Which made me laugh harder, and I said, "I love you."

And my sister said, "I love you, too. Just stop it with the laughing already."

Eventually, my laughing turned into the occasional chuckle, and then it just stopped. I looked back and saw that my sister was asleep. So, I started the car and turned on the heater, so she would be warm. That's when I started reading the book Bill gave me. It's *Walden* by Henry David Thoreau, which is my brother's girlfriend's favorite book, so I was very excited to read it.

▷ **63** *crack the window* (AE infml): open the window a little **69** *chuckle* (n): low short laugh

When the sun went down, I put my smoking pamphlet on the page where I stopped reading and started driving home. I stopped a few blocks from our house to wake up my sister and put the blanket and pillow in the trunk. We pulled into the driveway. We got out. We went inside. And we heard our mother and father's voices from the top of the stairs.

"Where have you two been all day?"

"Yeah. Dinner's almost ready."

My sister looked at me. I looked at her. She shrugged. So, I started talking a mile a minute about how we saw a movie and how my sister taught me how to drive on the highways and how we went to McDonald's.

"McDonald's?! When?!"

"Your mother cooked ribs, you know?" My father was reading the paper.

As I talked, my sister went up to my father and gave him a kiss on the cheek. He didn't look up from his paper.

"I know, but we didn't go to McDonald's until before the movie, and that was a while ago."

Then, my father said matter-of-factly, "What movie did you see?"

I froze, but my sister came through with the name of a movie just before she kissed my mother on the cheek. I had never heard of this movie.

"Was it any good?"

I froze again.

My sister was so calm. "It was okay. Those ribs smell great."

"Yeah," I said. Then, I thought of something to change the subject. "Hey, Dad. Is the hockey game on tonight?"

"Yeah, but you're only allowed to watch it with me if you don't ask any of your stupid questions."

"Okay, but can I ask one now before it starts?"

"I don't know. Can you?"

"May I?" I asked, corrected.

He grunted, "Go ahead."

"What do the players call a hockey puck again?"

"A biscuit. They call it a biscuit."

"Great. Thanks."

From that moment and all through dinner, my parents didn't ask any more questions about our day, although my mom did say how glad she was that my sister and I were spending more time together.

That night, after our parents went to sleep, I went down to the car and got the pillow and blanket out of the trunk. I brought them to my sister in her room. She was pretty tired. And she spoke very softly. She thanked me for the whole day. She said that I didn't let her down. And she said that she wanted it to be our little secret since she decided to tell her old boyfriend that the pregnancy was a false alarm. I guess she just didn't trust him with the truth anymore.

Just after I turned out the lights and opened the door, I heard her say softly,

"I want you to stop smoking, you hear?"

"I hear."

"Because I really do love you, Charlie."

"I love you, too."

"I mean it."

"So do I."

"Okay, then. Good night."

"Good night."

That's when I shut the door and left her to sleep.

I didn't feel like reading that night, so I went downstairs and watched a half-hour-long commercial that advertised an exercise machine. They kept flashing a 1-800 number, so I called it. The woman who picked up the other end of the phone was named Michelle. And I told Michelle that I was a kid and did not need an exercise machine, but I hoped she was having a good night.

That's when Michelle hung up on me. And I didn't mind a bit.

Love always,
Charlie

March 7, 1992

Dear friend,

Girls are weird, and I don't mean that offensively. I just can't put it any other way.

I have now gone on another date with Mary Elizabeth. In a lot of ways, it was similar to the dance except that we got to wear more comfortable clothes. She was the one who asked me out again, and I suppose that's okay, but I think I'm going to start doing the asking from time to time because I can't always hope to get asked. Also, if I do the asking, then I'll be sure to go out with the girl of my choice if she says yes. It's just so complicated.

The good news is that I got to be the one who drove this time. I asked my father if I could borrow his car. It happened at the dinner table.

"What for?" My dad gets protective of his car.

"Charlie's got a girlfriend," my sister said.

"She's not my girlfriend," I said.

"Who is this girl?" my father asked.

"What's going on?" my mother asked from the kitchen.

"Charlie wants to borrow the car," my dad replied.

"What for?" my mother asked.

"That's what I'm trying to find out!" my father said with a raised voice.

"No need to get snippy," my mother said.

"Sorry," my father said without meaning it. Then, he turned back to me.

"So, tell me about this girl."

So, I told him a little about Mary Elizabeth, leaving out the part about the tattoo and belly button ring. He kind of smiled for a little while, trying to see if I was already guilty of something. Then, he said yes. I could borrow his car. When my mother came in with coffee, my father told her the whole story while I ate dessert.

That night, as I was finishing my book, my father came in and sat on the edge of my bed. He lit a cigarette and started telling me about sex. He gave me this talk a few years before, but it was more biological then. Now, he was saying things like …

"I know I'm your old man, but … "

"you can't be too careful these days," and

"wear protection," and

"if she says no, then you have to assume she means it … "

"because if you force her to do something she doesn't want to do, then you're in big trouble, mister … "

"and even if she says no, and really means yes, then quite frankly she's playing games and isn't worth the price of dinner."

"if you need to talk to somebody, you can come to me, but if you don't want to do that for some reason, talk to your brother," and finally

"I'm glad we had this talk."

Then, my father ruffled my hair, smiled, and left the room. I guess I should tell you that my father isn't like on television. Things like sex don't embarrass him. And he is actually very smart about them.

I think he was especially happy because I used to kiss this boy in the neighborhood a lot when I was very little, and even though the psychiatrist said it was very natural for little boys and girls to explore things like that, I think my father was afraid anyway. I guess that's natural, but I'm not sure why.

Anyway, Mary Elizabeth and I went to see a movie downtown. It was what they call an "art" movie. Mary Elizabeth said it won an award at some big film festival in Europe, and she thought that was impressive. As we waited for the movie to start, she said what a shame it was that so many people would go to see a stupid Hollywood movie, but there were only a few people in this theater. Then, she talked about how she couldn't wait to get out of here and go to college where people appreciate things like that.

Then the movie started. It was in a foreign language and had subtitles, which was fun because I had never read a movie before. The movie itself was very interesting, but I didn't think it was very good because I didn't really feel different when it was over.

But Mary Elizabeth felt different. She kept saying it was an "articulate" film. So "articulate." And I guess it was. The thing is, I didn't know what it said even if it said it very well.

Later, I drove us to this underground record store, and Mary Elizabeth gave me a tour. She loves this record store. She said it was the one place where she felt like herself. She said that before coffee

▷ **24** *snippy* (infml): rude, bad-tempered **70** *articulate* [ɑːrˈtɪkjələt] (adj): good at expressing ideas and feelings clearly and intelligently

shops were popular, there was nowhere for kids like her to go, except the Big Boy, and that was old until this year.

She showed me the movie section and told me about all these cult filmmakers and people from France. Then, she took me down to the import section and told me about "real" alternative music. Then, she took me to the folk section and told me about girl bands like the Slits.

She said she felt really bad she hadn't gotten me anything for Christmas, and she wanted to make it up to me. Then, she bought me a record by Billie Holiday and asked if I wanted to go to her house and listen to it.

So, I was sitting alone in her basement while she was upstairs getting us something to drink. And I looked around the room, which was very clean and smelled like people didn't live there. It had a fireplace with a mantel and golf trophies. And there was a television and a nice stereo. And then Mary Elizabeth came downstairs with two glasses and a bottle of brandy. She said that she hated everything her parents loved, except for brandy.

She asked me to pour the drinks while she made a fire. She was very excited, too, which was strange because she's never like that. She kept talking about how much she loves fires and how she wanted to marry a man and live in Vermont someday, which was strange, too, because Mary Elizabeth never talks about things like that. When she finished the fire, she put on the record, and kind of danced over to me. She said she felt very warm, but not in the temperature sense.

The music started, and she clinked my glass, said "cheers," and took a sip of brandy. Brandy is very good, by the way, but it was better at the Secret Santa party. We finished the first glasses very quickly.

My heart was beating really fast, and I was starting to get nervous. She handed me another glass of brandy and touched my hand very softly when she did it. Then, she slipped her leg over mine, and I watched it just dangle there. Then, I felt her hand on the back of my neck. Just kind of moving slowly. And my heart started beating crazy.

"Do you like the record?" she asked real quiet.

"Very much." I really did, too. It was beautiful.

"Charlie?"

"Uh-huh?"

"Do you like me?"

"Uh-huh."

"You know what I mean?"

"Uh-huh."

"Are you nervous?"

"Uh-huh."

"Don't be nervous."

"Okay."

That's when I felt her other hand. It started at my knee and worked its way up the side of my leg to my hip and stomach. Then, she took her leg off mine and kind of sat on my lap facing me. She looked right into my eyes, and she never blinked. Not once. Her face looked warm and different. And she leaned down and started kissing my neck and ears. Then my cheeks. Then my lips. And everything kind of melted away. She took my hand and slid it up her sweater, and I couldn't believe what was happening to me. Or what breasts felt like. Or later, what they looked like. Or how difficult bras are.

After we had done everything you can do from the stomach up, I lay down on the floor, and Mary Elizabeth put her head on my chest. We both breathed very slowly and listened to the music and the fire crack. When the last song was over, I felt her breath on my chest.

"Charlie?"

"Uh-huh?"

"Do you think I'm pretty?"

"I think you're very pretty."

"Really?"

"Really."

Then, she held on to me a little tighter, and for the next half hour, Mary Elizabeth didn't talk at all. All I could do was lie there and think about how much her voice changed when she asked me if she was pretty, and how much she changed when I answered, and how Sam said she didn't like things like that, and how much my arm was beginning to hurt.

Thank God we heard the automatic garage door opener when we did.

Love always,
Charlie

▷ **6** *the Slits:* UK girl punk band (1976–1981) **9** *Billie Holiday* (1915–1959): American black jazz singer **14** *mantel:* shelf above a fireplace where objects can be displayed **21** *Vermont:* north-eastern state of the USA **53** *bra:* piece of women's underwear worn to cover and support the breast

March 28, 1992

Dear friend,

It's finally starting to get a little warm here, and the people are being nicer in the hallways. Not to me necessarily, just in a general way. I wrote a paper about *Walden* for Bill, but this time I did it differently. I didn't write a book report. I wrote a report pretending that I was by myself near a lake for two years. I pretended that I lived off the land and had insights. To tell you the truth, I kind of like the idea of doing that right now.

Ever since that night with Mary Elizabeth, everything has been different. It started out that Monday in school where Sam and Patrick looked at me with big grins. Mary Elizabeth had told them about the night we spent together, which I really didn't want her to do, but Sam and Patrick thought it was great, and they were really happy for both of us. Sam kept saying,

"I can't believe I didn't think of it before. You guys are great together."

I think Mary Elizabeth thinks so, too, because she's been acting completely different. She's nice all the time, but it doesn't feel right. I don't know how to describe it. It's like we'll be having a cigarette outside with Sam and Patrick at the end of the day, and we'll all be talking about something until it's time to go home. Then, when I get home, Mary Elizabeth will call me right away and ask me, "What's up?" And I don't know what to say because the only thing new in my life is my walk home, which isn't a lot. But I describe the walk anyway. And then she starts talking, and she doesn't stop for a long time. She's been doing this all week. That and picking lint off my clothes.

At one point two days ago, she was talking about books, and she included a lot of books I had read. And when I told her that I had read them, she asked me very long questions that were really just her ideas with a question mark put at the end. The only thing I could say was either "yes" or "no." There was honestly no room to say anything else. After that, she started talking about her plans for college, which I had heard before, so I put down the phone, went to the bathroom, and when I came back, she was still talking. I know that was the wrong thing to do, but I thought if I didn't take a break, I would do something even worse. Like yell or hang up the phone.

She also keeps talking about the Billie Holiday record she bought for me. And she says she wants to expose me to all these great things. And to tell you the truth, I don't really want to be exposed to all these great things if it means that I'll have to hear Mary Elizabeth talk about all the great things she exposed me to all the time. It almost feels like of the three things involved: Mary Elizabeth, me, and the great things, only the first one matters to Mary Elizabeth. I don't understand that. I would give someone a record so they could love the record, not so they would always know that I gave it to them.

Then, there was the dinner. Since the holidays were over, my mom asked if I would like to have Sam and Patrick over for dinner like she promised after I told her they said she had great taste in clothing. I was so excited! I told Patrick and Sam, and we made plans for a Sunday night, and about two hours later, Mary Elizabeth walked up to me in the hall, and said,

"What time Sunday?"

I didn't know what to do. It was just for Sam and Patrick. That was the whole idea from the beginning. And I never even invited Mary Elizabeth. I guess I know why she assumed that she would be invited, but she never even waited to see. Or even drop a hint. Or anything.

So, at the dinner, the dinner where I wanted my mom and dad to see how nice and great Sam and Patrick were, Mary Elizabeth talked the whole time. It wasn't all her fault. My dad and mom asked her more questions than they asked Sam or Patrick. I guess because I am going on dates with Mary Elizabeth, and that is more curious to them than my friends are. I guess that makes sense. But still. It's like they never got to meet Sam and Patrick. And that was the whole point. By the time dinner was over, and they all left, all my mom said was that Mary Elizabeth was smart, and all my dad said was my "girlfriend" was pretty. They didn't say anything about Sam or Patrick. And all I wanted from the whole night was for them to know my friends. That was very important to me.

Sex things are weird, too. It's like after that first night, we have this pattern where we basically do what we did that first time, but there is no fire or Billie Holiday record because we are in a car, and everything

▷ **27** *lint* (BE: *fluff*): very small pieces of cotton, wool, etc. that stick to a person's clothing

is rushed. Maybe this is the way things are supposed to be, but it doesn't feel right.

My sister has been reading all these books about women ever since she told her ex-boyfriend that the pregnancy was a false alarm, and he wanted to get back together, and she said no.

So, I asked her about Mary Elizabeth (leaving out the sex part) because I knew she could be neutral about it, especially since she "stayed clear" of the dinner. My sister said Mary Elizabeth is suffering from low self-esteem, but I told her that she said the same thing about Sam back in November when she started dating Craig, and Sam is completely different. Everything can't be low self-esteem, can it?

My sister tried to clarify things. She said that by introducing me to all these great things, Mary Elizabeth gained a "superior position" that she wouldn't need if she was confident about herself. She also said that people who try to control situations all the time are afraid that if they don't, nothing will work out the way they want.

I don't know if this is right or not, but it made me sad regardless. Not for Mary Elizabeth. Or for me. Just in general. Because I started to think that I didn't know who Mary Elizabeth was at all. I'm not saying she was lying to me, but she just acted so different before I got to know her, and if she really isn't like what she was at the beginning, I wish she could have just said so. But maybe she is like she was at the beginning, and I just didn't realize it. I just don't want to be another thing Mary Elizabeth is in charge of.

I asked my sister what I should do, and she said the best thing to do is be honest about my feelings. My psychiatrist said the same thing. And then I felt really sad because I thought maybe I was different from how Mary Elizabeth originally saw me, too. And maybe I was lying by not telling her that it was hard to listen to her all the time without getting to say anything back. But I was just trying to be nice like Sam said I should. I don't know where I went wrong.

I tried to call my brother about this, but his roommate said he was really busy with school, so I decided not to leave a message because I didn't want to distract him. The one thing I did was mail my report about *Walden* to him, so he could share it with his girlfriend. Then, maybe if they had time, they could read it, and we could talk about it, and I would have the chance to ask them both what to do about Mary Elizabeth since they were going out in a good way and would know how to make things work. Even if we didn't get to talk about it, I would still love to meet my brother's girlfriend. Even on the phone. I did get to see her once on a VCR tape of one of my brother's football games, but it's really not the same thing. Even though she was very beautiful. But not in an unconventional way. I don't know why I'm saying all this. I just wish Mary Elizabeth would ask me questions other than "What's up?"

Love always,
Charlie

April 18, 1992

Dear friend,

I have made a terrible mess of things. I really have. I feel terrible about it. Patrick said the best thing I could do is just stay away for a while.

It all started last Monday. Mary Elizabeth came to school with a book of poems by a famous poet named e. e. cummings. The story behind the book was that she saw a movie that talked about one poem that compares this woman's hands to flowers and rain. She thought it was so beautiful that she went out and bought the book. She has read it a lot of times since, and she said she wanted me to have my own copy. Not the copy she bought, but a new one.

All day she told me to show everyone the book.

I know I should have been grateful because it was a very nice thing to do. But I wasn't grateful. I wasn't grateful at all. Don't get me wrong. I acted like I was. But I wasn't. To tell you the truth, I was starting to get mad. Maybe if she would have given me the copy of the book that she bought for herself, it would have been different. Or maybe if she had just hand-copied the rain poem she loves on a piece of nice paper. And definitely if she didn't make me show the book to everyone we know.

▷ **8** *stay clear of sth.:* (here) not be present at sth. **24** *be in charge of sth.:* have control over sth. **54** *e.e. cummings* (1894–1962): American modernist poet **55** *movie:* reference to *Hannah and Her Sisters* (1986) by Woody Allen, in which cumming's poem "somewhere I have never travelled" is quoted

Maybe I should have been honest then, but it didn't feel like the right time.

When I left school that day, I didn't go home because I just couldn't talk to her on the phone, and my mother is not a very "adroit" liar about things like that. So, instead, I walked to the area where all the shops and video stores are. I went straight to the bookstore. And when the lady behind the counter asked me if I needed any help, I opened up my bag, and I returned the book Mary Elizabeth bought me. I didn't do anything with the money. It just sat in my pocket.

When I walked home, all I could think was what a terrible thing it was that I just did, and I started crying. By the time I walked in the front door, I was crying so much that my sister stopped watching television to talk to me. When I told her what I did, she drove me back to the bookstore because I was too messy to drive, and I got the book back, which made me feel a little better.

When Mary Elizabeth asked me where I had been all day on the phone that night, I told her that I went to the store with my sister. And when she asked if I bought her something nice, I said I did. I didn't even think she was serious, but I said it anyway. I just felt so bad about almost returning her book. I spent the next hour on the phone listening to her talk about the book. Then, we said good night. Then, I went downstairs to ask my sister if she could drive me to the store again, so I could get Mary Elizabeth something nice. My sister told me to drive myself. And that I had better start being honest with Mary Elizabeth about how I feel. Maybe I should have then, but it just didn't feel like the right time.

The next day in school I gave Mary Elizabeth the gift that I drove to buy her. It was a new copy of *To Kill a Mockingbird*. The first thing Mary Elizabeth said was,

"That's original."

I just reminded myself that she didn't say it mean. She wasn't making fun of me. She wasn't comparing. Or criticizing. And she really wasn't. Believe me. So, I just explained to her how Bill gives me special books to read outside of class and how *To Kill a Mockingbird* was the first one. And how it was special to me. Then, she said,

"Thank you. It's very sweet."

But then she went on to explain how she had read it three years earlier and thought it was "overrated" and how they turned it into a black-and-white film with famous actors like Gregory Peck and

Robert Duvall that won an Academy Award for the screenplay writer. I just kind of put my feelings away somewhere after that.

I left school, walked around, and didn't get home until one o'clock in the morning. When I explained to my father why, he told me to act like a man.

The next day in school, when Mary Elizabeth asked where I had been the day before, I told her that I bought a pack of cigarettes, went to the Big Boy, and spent the entire day reading the e. e. cummings book and eating club sandwiches. I knew I was safe saying that because she would never ask me any questions about the book. And I was right. After she got done talking about it that time, I didn't think I'd ever really need to read it myself. Even if I wanted to.

I definitely think I should have been honest then, but to tell you the truth, I was getting as mad as I used to get playing sports, and it was starting to scare me.

Luckily, Easter vacation was starting on Friday, and it distracted things a little bit. Bill gave me *Hamlet* to read for the break. He said I would need the free time to really concentrate on the play. I guess I don't need to say who wrote it. The only advice Bill gave me was to think about the main character in terms of the other main characters in the books I've read thus far. He said not to get caught up thinking the play was "too fancy."

So, on Good Friday yesterday, we had a special showing of *The Rocky Horror Picture Show*. What made it special was the fact that everyone knew it was the beginning of Easter vacation, and a lot of kids were still wearing their suits and dresses from Mass. It reminded me of Ash Wednesday in school when the kids come in with thumbprints on their foreheads. It always adds an air of excitement.

After the show, Craig invited all of us back to his apartment to drink wine and listen to the White Album. After the record was over, Patrick suggested we all play truth or dare, a game that he loves to play when he's "buzzed."

▷ **4** *adroit* [əˈdrɔɪt]: clever **31** *mean* (adv): in a nasty way **38** *overrate sth.:* think too highly of sth. **59** *in terms of sth.:* by thinking about sth. **61** *fancy* (infml): (here) literary; too far from your own experience **62** *Good Friday:* Karfreitag **66–67** *with thumbprints on their foreheads:* in the Catholic church, believers are given a mark of ashes on their foreheads on Ash Wednesday **69** *White Album:* record (1968) by the Beatles **70** *dare* (n): Mutprobe **71** *buzzed* (infml): slightly drunk or on drugs

Guess who chose dares over truth all night? Me. I just didn't want to tell Mary Elizabeth the truth because of a game.

It was working pretty well most of the night. The dares were things like "chug a beer." But then, Patrick gave me a dare. I don't even think he knew what he was doing, but he gave it to me anyway.

"Kiss the prettiest girl in the room on the lips."

That's when I chose to be honest. In retrospect, I probably could not have picked a worse time.

The silence started after I stood up (since Mary Elizabeth was sitting right next to me). By the time I had knelt down in front of Sam and kissed her, the silence was unbearable. It wasn't a romantic kiss. It was friendly, like when I played Rocky and she played Janet. But it didn't matter.

I could say that it was the wine or the beer that I chugged. I could also say that I had forgotten the time Mary Elizabeth asked me if I thought she was pretty. But I would be lying. The truth is that when Patrick dared me, I knew that if I kissed Mary Elizabeth, I would be lying to everyone. Including Sam. Including Patrick. Including Mary Elizabeth. And I just couldn't do it anymore. Even if it was part of a game.

After the silence, Patrick did his best to salvage the evening. The first thing he said was,

"Well, isn't this awkward?"

But it didn't work. Mary Elizabeth walked quickly out of the room and into the bathroom. Patrick told me later that she didn't want anyone to see her cry. Sam followed her, but before she completely left the room, she turned to me and said serious and dark,

"What the fuck is wrong with you?"

It was the look on her face when she said it. And how much she meant it. It suddenly made everything seem like it really was. I felt terrible. Just terrible. Patrick immediately stood up and took me out of Craig's apartment. We walked to the street, and the only thing I was aware of was the cold. I said that I should go back inside and apologize. Patrick said,

"No. I'll get our coats. Just stay here."

When Patrick left me outside, I started to cry. It was real and panicky, and I couldn't stop it. When Patrick came back, I said, really crying,

"I really think I should go apologize."

Patrick shook his head. "Believe me. You don't want to go in there."

Then, he jiggled the car keys in front of my face and said, "Come on. I'll take you home."

In the car, I told Patrick everything that had been going on. About the record. And the book. And *To Kill a Mockingbird*. And how Mary Elizabeth never asked any questions. And all Patrick said was, "It's too bad you're not gay."

That made me stop crying a little bit.

"Then again, if you were gay, I would never date you. You're a mess."

That made me start laughing a little bit.

"And I thought Brad was fucked-up. Jesus."

That made me laugh a lot more. Then, he turned on the radio and we drove through the tunnels back home. When he dropped me off, Patrick told me the best thing to do was keep away for a while. I guess I already told you that. He said that when he knew more, he'd give me a call.

"Thanks, Patrick."

"Don't mention it."

And then I said, "You know, Patrick? If I were gay, I'd want to date you."

I don't know why I said it, but it seemed right.

Patrick just smiled cocky and said, "Of course." Then, he peeled out down the road.

When I lay down in bed that night, I put on the Billie Holiday record, and I started reading the book of e. e. cummings poems. After I read the poem that compares the woman's hands to flowers and rain, I put the book down and went to the window. I stared at my reflection and the trees behind it for a long time. Not thinking anything. Not feeling anything. Not hearing the record. For hours.

Something really is wrong with me. And I don't know what it is.

Love always,
Charlie

▷ **4** *chug sth.* (AE sl): drink sth. all at once **7** *in retrospect:* looking back **21** *salvage sth.:* try to save sth. **23** *awkward* ['ɔːkwərd]: embarrassing **62** *cocky* (adv, infml): in a self-confident way that is annoying **62–63** *peel out* (infml): drive off quickly

April 26, 1992

Dear friend,

Nobody has called me since that night. I don't blame them. I have spent the whole vacation reading *Hamlet*. Bill was right. It was much easier to think of the kid in the play like the other characters I've read about so far. It has also helped me while I'm trying to figure out what's wrong with me. It didn't give me any answers necessarily, but it was helpful to know that someone else has been through it. Especially someone who lived such a long time ago.

I did call Mary Elizabeth, and I told her that I'd been listening to the record every night and reading the e. e. cummings book.

She just said, "It's too late, Charlie."

I would have explained that I didn't want to start going on dates again and I was just doing these things as a friend, but I knew it would have only made things worse, so I didn't.

I just said, "I'm sorry."

And I really was sorry. And I know that she believed me. But when that didn't make any difference, and there was nothing but a bad silence on the phone, I really knew it was too late.

Patrick did call me, but all he said was that Craig got really angry at Sam about me, and I should keep staying away until things got clear. I asked him if he would like to go out, just him and me. He said that he would be busy with Brad and family things, but he'd try to call me if he could find the time. So far, he hasn't.

I would tell you about Easter Sunday with my family, but I've already told you about Thanksgiving and Christmas, and there really isn't much of a difference.

Except that my father got a raise, and my mother didn't because she doesn't get paid for housework, and my sister stopped reading those self-esteem books because she met a new boy.

My brother did come home, but when I asked him if his girlfriend read my report on *Walden*, he said no because she broke up with him when she found out he was cheating on her. That happened a while ago. So, I asked him if he had read it himself, and he said that he hadn't because he was too busy. He said he would try to read it over vacation. So far, he hasn't.

So, I went to visit my aunt Helen, and for the first time in my life, it didn't help. I even tried to follow my own plan and remember all the details about the last time I had a great week, but that didn't help, either.

I know that I brought this all on myself. I know that I deserve this. I'd do anything not to be this way. I'd do anything to make it up to everyone. And to not have to see a psychiatrist, who explains to me about being "passive aggressive." And to not have to take the medicine he gives me, which is too expensive for my dad. And to not have to talk about bad memories with him. Or be nostalgic about bad things.

I just wish that God or my parents or Sam or my sister or someone would just tell me what's wrong with me. Just tell me how to be different in a way that makes sense. To make this all go away. And disappear. I know that's wrong because it's my responsibility, and I know that things get worse before they get better because that's what my psychiatrist says, but this is a worse that feels too big.

After a week of not talking to anyone, I finally called Bob. I know that's wrong, but I didn't know what else to do. I asked him if he had anything I could buy. He said he had a quarter ounce of pot left. So, I took some of my Easter money and bought it.

I've been smoking it all the time since.

Love always,
Charlie

▷ **28** *raise* (n): more money for your work **33** *cheat on sb.*: have sex with a person while still being officially together with sb. else

part

4

April 29, 1992

Dear friend,

I wish I could report that it's getting better, but unfortunately it isn't. It's hard, too, because we've started school again, and I can't go to the places where I used to go. And it can't be like it was. And I wasn't ready to say good-bye just yet.

To tell you the truth, I've just been avoiding everything.

I walk around the school hallways and look at the people. I look at the teachers and wonder why they're here. If they like their jobs. Or us. And I wonder how smart they were when they were fifteen. Not in a mean way. In a curious way. It's like looking at all the students and wondering who's had their heart broken that day, and how they are able to cope with having three quizzes and a book report on top of that. Or wondering who did the heart breaking. And wondering why. Especially since I know that if they went to another school, the person who had their heart broken would have had their heart broken by somebody else, so why does it have to be so personal? And if I went to another school, I would never have known Sam or Patrick or Mary Elizabeth or anyone except my family.

I can tell you one thing that happened. I was in the shopping mall because that's where I go lately. For the last couple of weeks, I've been going there every day, trying to figure out why people go there. It's kind of a personal project.

There was this one little boy. He might have been four years old. I'm not sure. He was crying really hard, and he kept screaming for his mom. He must have been lost. Then, I saw this older kid, who was maybe seventeen. I think he went to a different school because I had never seen him before. Anyway, this older kid, who was really tough-looking with a leather jacket and long hair and everything, went up to the little boy and asked him what his name was. The little boy answered and stopped crying.

Then, the older kid walked away with the little boy.

A minute later, I heard the intercom say to the mom that her boy was at the information desk. So, I went to the information desk to see what would happen.

I guess the mom had been searching for the little boy for a long time because she came running up to the information desk, and when she saw the little boy, she started crying. She held him tightly and told him to never run off again. Then, she thanked the older kid who had helped, and all the older kid said was, "Next time just watch him a little fucking better."

Then, he walked away.

The man with the moustache behind the information desk was speechless. So was the mom. The little boy just wiped his nose, looked up at his mom, and said,

"French fries."

The mom looked down at the little boy and nodded, and they left. So, I followed them. They went to the place where the food stands are, and they got french fries. The little boy was smiling and getting ketchup all over himself. And the mom kept wiping his face in between taking drags off her cigarette.

I kept looking at the mom, trying to imagine what she must have looked like when she was young. If she was married. If her little boy was an accident or planned. And if that made a difference.

I saw other people there. Old men sitting alone. Young girls with blue eye shadow and awkward jaws. Little kids who looked tired. Fathers in nice coats who looked even more tired. Kids working behind the counters of the food places who looked like they hadn't had the will to live for hours. The machines kept opening and closing. The people kept giving money and getting their change. And it all felt very unsettling to me.

So, I decided to find another place to go and figure out why people go there. Unfortunately, there aren't a lot of places like that. I don't know how much longer I can keep going without a friend. I used to be able to do it very easily, but that was before I knew what having a friend was like. It's much easier not to know things sometimes. And to have french fries with your mom be enough.

The only person I've really talked to in the last two weeks was Susan, the girl who used to "go with" Michael back in middle school when she had braces. I saw her standing in the hall, surrounded by a group of boys I didn't know. They were all laughing and making sex jokes, and Susan was doing her best to laugh along with them. When she saw me approaching the group, her face went "ashen." It was

▷ **13** *quiz:* (cf. p. 182) **28–29** *tough-looking:* physically strong and likely not to be sensitive **51** *drag* (n, infml): act of breathing in the smoke of a cigarette quickly **56** *jaw:* Kiefer **61** *unsettling:* making you feel upset, nervous or worried

almost like she didn't want to remember what she was like twelve months ago, and she certainly didn't want the boys to know that she knew me and used to be my friend. The whole group got quiet and stared at me, but I didn't even notice them. I just looked at Susan, and all I said was,

"Do you ever miss him?"

I didn't say it mean or accusingly. I just wanted to know if anybody else remembered Michael. To tell you the truth, I was stoned in a bad way, and I couldn't get the question out of my mind.

Susan was at a loss. She didn't know what to do. These were the first words we had spoken since the end of last year. I guess it wasn't fair of me to ask her in a group like that, but I never see her by herself anymore, and I really needed to know.

At first, I thought her blank expression was the result of surprise, but after it didn't go away for a long while, I knew that it wasn't. It suddenly dawned on me that if Michael were still around, Susan probably wouldn't be "going out" with him anymore. Not because she's a bad person or shallow or mean. But because things change. And friends leave. And life doesn't stop for anybody.

"I'm sorry I bothered you, Susan. I'm just having a tough time. That's all. Have a good one," I said and walked away.

"God, that kid is such a fucking freak," I heard one of the boys whisper when I was halfway down the hall. He said it more factual than mean, and Susan didn't correct him. I don't know if I would have corrected him myself these days.

Love always,
Charlie

May 2, 1992

Dear friend,

A few days ago, I went to see Bob to buy more pot. I should probably say that I keep forgetting Bob doesn't go to school with us. Probably because he watches more television than anyone I know, and he's great with trivia. You should see him talk about Mary Tyler Moore. It's kind of spooky.

Bob has this very specific way of living. He says he takes a shower every other day. He weighs his "stash" daily. He says when you're smoking a cigarette with someone, and you have a lighter, you should light their cigarette first. But if you have matches, you should light your cigarette first, so you breathe in the "harmful sulfur" instead of them. He says it's the polite thing to do. He also says that it's bad luck to have "three on a match." He heard that from his uncle who fought in Vietnam. Something about how three cigarettes was enough time for the enemy to know where you are.

Bob says that when you're alone, and you light a cigarette, and the cigarette is only halfway lit that means someone is thinking about you. He also says that when you find a penny, it's only "lucky" if it's heads-up. He says the best thing to do is find a lucky penny when you're with someone and give the other person the good luck. He believes in karma. He also loves to play cards.

Bob goes part-time to the local community college. He wants to be a chef. He is an only child, and his parents are never home. He says it used to bother him a lot when he was younger, but not so much anymore.

The thing about Bob is that when you first meet him, he's really interesting because he knows about cigarette rules and pennies and Mary Tyler Moore. But after you've known him for a while, he starts to repeat these things. In the last few weeks, he hasn't said anything that I haven't heard from him before. That's what made it such a shock when he told me what happened.

Basically, Brad's father caught Brad and Patrick together.

I guess that Brad's father didn't know about his son because when he caught them, Brad's father started beating Brad. Not a slap kind of beating. A belt kind. A real kind. Patrick told Sam who told Bob that he had never seen anything like it. I guess it was that bad. He wanted

▷ **10** *be at a loss:* not know what to say or do **14** *blank* (adj): showing no feeling, understanding or interest **15–16** *it dawned on sb. that …:* sb. realized for the first time that … **18** *shallow:* superficial, without depth **21** *one:* (here) day **33** *trivia:* unimportant matters **33–34** *Mary Tyler Moore* (born 1936): star of the TV sitcom *The Mary Tyler Moore Show* (1970–1977) **34** *spooky* (infml): scary **36** *stash* (infml): secret supply of sth. (here, drugs) **39** *sulphur:* Schwefel **47** *heads-up:* with the side of a coin that has the picture of a person on it upwards **49** *karma:* (in Buddhism and Hinduism) fate, destiny **50** *community college:* (cf. p. 181) **51** *chef:* professional cook

to say "Stop" and "You're killing him." He even wanted to hold Brad's father down. But he just froze. And Brad kept yelling, "Get out!" to Patrick. And finally, Patrick just did.

That was last week. And Brad still hasn't come to school. Everyone thinks he might have been sent to a military school or something. Nobody knows for sure about anything. Patrick tried calling once, but when Brad's father answered, he just hung up.

Bob said Patrick was "in bad shape." I can't tell you how sad I felt when he told me that because I wanted to call Patrick and be his friend and help him. But I didn't know if I should call him because of what he had said about waiting until things got clear. The thing was I couldn't think about anything else.

So, on Friday, I went to *The Rocky Horror Picture Show*. I waited until the movie had already started before I went into the theater. I didn't want to ruin the show for everybody. I just wanted to see Patrick play Frank 'N Furter just like he always does because I knew that if I saw that, I knew he would be okay. Just like my sister getting mad at me for smoking cigarettes.

I sat in the back row and looked on the stage. It was still a couple of scenes before Frank 'N Furter enters. That's when I saw Sam playing Janet. And I missed her so much. And I was so sorry about how I messed everything up. Especially when I saw Mary Elizabeth playing Magenta. It was all very hard to watch. But then Patrick finally came on as Frank 'N Furter, and he was great. He was actually better than ever in a lot of ways. It was just so nice to see all my friends. I left before the movie was over.

I drove home listening to some of the songs we listened to those times when we were infinite. And I pretended they were in the car with me. I even talked out loud. I told Patrick how I thought he was great. I asked Sam about Craig. I told Mary Elizabeth that I was sorry and how much I really loved the e. e. cummings book and wanted to ask her questions about it. But then I stopped because it started to make me too sad. I also thought that if anybody saw me talking out loud when I was alone in the car, their looks might convince me that the something that's wrong with me might be even worse than I thought.

When I got home, my sister was watching a movie with her new boyfriend. There isn't much to say other than his name is Erik, and he has short hair and is a junior. Erik had rented the movie. After I shook hands with him, I asked them about the movie because I didn't recognize it except for an actor who used to be on a TV show, and I couldn't remember his name.

My sister said, "It's stupid. You wouldn't like it."

I said, "What's it about?"

She said, "Come on, Charlie. It's almost over."

I said, "Would it be okay if I watched the end?"

She said, "You can watch it when we're done."

I said, "Well, how about I watch the end with you, and then I can rewind it and watch up to the point I started watching with you?"

That's when she paused the movie.

"Can't you take a hint?"

"I suppose not."

"We want to be alone, Charlie."

"Oh. I'm sorry."

To tell you the truth, I knew she wanted to be alone with Erik, but I really wanted to have some company. I knew it wasn't fair, though, to ruin her time just because I miss everybody, so I just said good night and left.

I went up to my room and started reading the new book Bill gave me. It's called *The Stranger*. Bill said that it's "very easy to read, but very hard to 'read well.'" I have no idea what he means, but I like the book so far.

Love always,
Charlie

May 8, 1992

Dear friend,

It's strange how things can change back as suddenly as they changed originally. When one thing happens and suddenly, things are back to normal.

▷ **5** *military school:* (cf. p. 182) **49** *rewind sth.* [ˌriːˈwaɪnd]: etwas zurückspulen **51** *take a hint:* understand what sb. wants you to do although he or she does not say it directly **60** *"The Stranger"* (French title: *L'Etranger*): novel (1942) by Albert Camus (1913–1960)

On Monday, Brad came back to school.

He looked very different. It wasn't that he was bruised or anything. His face actually looked fine. But before, Brad was always this guy who walked down the hallway with a bounce. I can't really describe it any other way. It's just that some people walk with their heads to the ground for some reason. They don't like to look other people in the eye. Brad was never like that. But now he is. Especially when it comes to Patrick.

I saw them talking quiet in the hallway. I was too far away to hear what they said, but I could tell that Brad was ignoring Patrick. And when Patrick started to get upset, Brad just closed his locker and walked away. It wasn't that strange because Brad and Patrick never talked in school since Brad wanted things to be secret. The strange part was that Patrick would walk up to Brad in the first place. So, I guessed that they didn't meet on the golf courses anymore. Or talk on the phone even.

Later that afternoon, I was having a cigarette outside by myself, and I saw Patrick alone, also having a cigarette. I wasn't close enough to really see him, but I didn't want to interfere with his personal time, so I didn't walk up to him. But Patrick was crying. He was crying pretty hard. After that, whenever I saw him around anywhere, he didn't look like he was there. He looked like he was someplace else. And I think I knew that because that's how people used to say I was. Maybe they still do. I'm not sure.

On Thursday, something really terrible happened.

I was sitting alone in the cafeteria, eating salisbury steak, when I saw Patrick walk up to Brad, who was sitting with his football buddies, and I saw Brad ignore him like he did at the locker. And I saw Patrick get really upset, but Brad still ignored him. Then, I saw Patrick say something, and he looked pretty angry as he turned to walk away. Brad sat still for a second, then he turned around. And then I heard it. It was just loud enough for a few tables to hear. The thing that Brad yelled at Patrick.

"Faggot!"

Brad's football buddies start laughing. A few tables got quiet as Patrick turned around. He was mad as hell. I'm not kidding. He stormed up to Brad's table and said,

"What did you call me?"

God, he was mad. I'd never seen Patrick like that before.

Brad sat quiet for a second, but his buddies kept egging him on by pushing his shoulders. Brad looked up at Patrick and said softer and meaner than the last time,

"I called you a faggot."

Brad's buddies started laughing even harder. That is, until Patrick threw the first punch. It's kind of eerie when a whole room gets quiet at once, and then the real noise starts.

The fight was hard. A lot harder than the one I had with Sean last year. There was no clean punching or things you see in movies. They just wrestled and hit. And whoever was the most aggressive or the most angry got in the most hits. In this case, it was pretty even until Brad's buddies got involved, and it became five on one.

That's when I got involved. I just couldn't watch them hurt Patrick even if things weren't clear just yet.

I think anyone who knew me might have been frightened or confused. Except maybe my brother. He taught me what to do in these situations. I don't really want to go into detail except to say that by the end of it, Brad and two of his buddies stopped fighting and just stared at me. His other two friends were lying on the ground. One was clutching the knee I bashed in with one of those metal cafeteria chairs. The other one was holding his face. I kind of swiped at his eyes, but not too bad. I didn't want to be too bad.

I looked down at the ground, and I saw Patrick. His face was pretty messed up, and he was crying hard. I helped him to his feet, and then I looked at Brad. I don't think we'd ever really exchanged two words before, but I guess this was the time to start. All I said was,

"If you ever do this again, I'll tell everyone. And if that doesn't work, I'll blind you."

I pointed at his friend who was holding his face, and I knew Brad heard me and knew that I meant it. He didn't say anything back, though, because the security guards of our school came to bring all of us out of the cafeteria. They took us first to the nurse, and then to Mr. Small. Patrick started the fight, so he was suspended for a week.

▷ **4** *with a bounce:* (here) energetically **26** *salisbury steak* ['sɑːlzbəri]: type of hamburger **34** *faggot* (derog sl): homosexual man **40** *egg sb. on:* encourage sb. to do sth. (esp. sth. which is unpleasant) **45** *eerie* ['ɪri; BE 'ɪəri]: strange and frightening **60** *swipe at sb./sth.:* hit or try to hit sb./sth.

Brad's buddies got three days each for ganging up on Patrick after they broke up the original fight. Brad wasn't suspended at all because it was self-defense. I didn't get suspended either because I was just helping to defend a friend when it was five on one.

Brad and I got a month's detention, starting that day.

In detention, Mr. Harris didn't set up any rules. He just let us read or do homework or talk. It really isn't much of a punishment unless you like the television programs right after school or are very concerned with your permanent record. I wonder if it's all a lie. A permanent record, I mean.

On that first day of detention, Brad came to sit next to me. He looked very sad. I think it all kind of hit him after he stopped feeling numb from the fight.

"Charlie?"

"Yeah?"

"Thanks. Thanks for stopping them."

"You're welcome."

And that was it. I haven't said anything to him since. And he didn't sit next to me today. At first when he said it, I was kind of confused. But then I think I got it. Because I wouldn't want a bunch of my friends beating up Sam even if I wasn't allowed to like her anymore either.

When I got out of detention that day, Sam was waiting for me. The minute I saw her, she smiled. I was numb. I just couldn't believe she was really there. Then, I saw her turn and give Brad a real cold look.

Brad said, "Tell him I'm sorry."

Sam replied, "Tell him yourself."

Brad looked away and walked to his car. Then, Sam walked up to me and messed up my hair.

"So, I heard you're this ninja or something."

I think I nodded.

Sam drove me home in her pickup truck. On the way, she told me that she was really angry at me for doing what I did to Mary Elizabeth. She told me that Mary Elizabeth is a really old friend of hers. She even reminded me that Mary Elizabeth was there for her when she went through that tough time she told me about when she gave me the typewriter. I don't really want to repeat what that was.

So, she said that when I kissed her instead of Mary Elizabeth, I really hurt their friendship for a while. Because I guess Mary

Elizabeth really liked me a lot. That made me feel sad because I didn't know that she liked me that much. I just thought she wanted to expose me to all those great things. That's when Sam said,

"Charlie, you're so stupid sometimes. Do you know that?"

"Yeah. I really do. Know that. Honest."

Then, she said that Mary Elizabeth and she got over it, and she thanked me for taking Patrick's advice and staying away for as long as I did because it made things easier. So, then I said,

"So, we can be friends now?"

"Of course," was all she said.

"And Patrick?"

"And Patrick."

"And everyone else?"

"And everyone else."

That's when I started crying. But Sam told me to shush.

"You remember what I said to Brad?"

"Yeah. You told him that he should tell Patrick that he was sorry himself."

"That goes for Mary Elizabeth, too."

"I tried, but she told me ... "

"I know you tried. I'm telling you to try again."

"Okay."

Sam dropped me off. When she was too far away to see me, I started to cry again. Because she was my friend again. And that was enough for me. So, I made myself promise to never mess up like I did before. And I'm never going to. I can tell you that.

When I went to *The Rocky Horror Picture Show* tonight, it was very tense. Not because of Mary Elizabeth. That was actually okay. I said I was sorry, and then I asked her if there was anything she wanted to say to me. And like before, I asked a question and got a very long answer. When I was done listening (I really did listen), I said I was sorry again. Then, she thanked me for not trying to make what I did seem less by offering a lot of excuses. And things were back to normal except we were just friends.

To tell you the truth, I think the biggest reason for everything being okay is that Mary Elizabeth started dating one of Craig's friends. His

▷ **5** *detention:* (cf. p. 181) **9** *permanent record:* (cf. p. 182) **13** *numb:* having no feelings **30** *ninja:* Japanese warrior **54** *shush* (infml): be quiet

name is Peter, and he's in college, which makes Mary Elizabeth happy. At the party at Craig's apartment, I overheard Mary Elizabeth say to Alice that she was much happier with Peter because he was "opinionated," and they had debates. She said that I was really sweet and understanding, but that our relationship was too one-sided. She wanted a person who was more open to discussion and didn't need someone's permission to talk.

I wanted to laugh. Or maybe get mad. Or maybe shrug at how strange everyone was, especially me. But I was at a party with my friends, so it really didn't matter that much. I just drank because I figured that it was about time to stop smoking so much pot.

The thing that made the evening tense was Patrick officially quit doing Frank 'N Furter in the show. He said that he didn't want to do it anymore ... ever. So, he sat and watched the show in the audience with me, and he said things that were hard to listen to because Patrick usually isn't unhappy.

"You ever think, Charlie, that our group is the same as any other group like the football team? And the only real difference between us is what we wear and why we wear it?"

"Yeah?" And there was this pause.

"Well, I think it's all bullshit."

And he meant it. It was hard to see him mean it that much.

Some guy that I didn't know from somewhere else did the part of Frank 'N Furter. He had been the second to Patrick for a long time, and now he got his chance. He was pretty good, too. Not as good as Patrick, but pretty good.

Love always,
Charlie

May 11, 1992

Dear friend,

I've been spending a lot of time with Patrick these days. I really haven't said much. I just kind of listen and nod because Patrick needs to talk. But it isn't like it was with Mary Elizabeth. It's different.

It started out on the Saturday morning after the show. I was in my bed trying to figure out why sometimes you can wake up and go back to sleep and other times you can't. Then, my mom knocked.

"Your friend Patrick's on the phone."

So, I got up and wiped away the sleep.

"Hello?"

"Get dressed. I'm on my way."

Click. That was it. I actually had a lot of work to do since it was getting closer to the end of the school year, but it sounded like we might be having some kind of adventure, so I got dressed anyway.

Patrick pulled up about ten minutes later. He was wearing the same clothes he wore the night before. He hadn't showered or anything. I don't even think he went to bed. He was just wide awake on coffee and cigarettes and Mini Thins, which are these small pills you can buy at Quick Marts or Truck Stops. They keep you awake! They're not illegal either, but they make you thirsty.

So, I climbed in Patrick's car, which was filled with cigarette smoke. He offered me one, but I said not in front of my house.

"Your parents don't know you smoke?"

"No. Should they?"

"I guess not."

Then, we started driving ... fast.

At first, Patrick didn't say much. He just listened to the music on the tape player. After the second song started, I asked him if it was the mix tape I made him for Secret Santa Christmas.

"I've been listening to it all night."

Patrick had this smile all over his face. It was a sick smile. Glazey and numb. He just turned up the volume. And drove faster.

"I'll tell you something, Charlie. I feel good. You know what I mean? Really good. Like I'm free or something. Like I don't have to pretend anymore. I'm going away to college, right? It'll be different there. You know what I mean?"

"Sure," I said.

"I've been thinking all night about what kind of posters I want to put up in my dorm room. And if I'll have an exposed brick wall. I've

▷ **8** *shrug at sth.:* lift your shoulders to show that you do not care about sth. **60** *glazey:* (here) without expression **68** *exposed:* uncovered

always wanted an exposed brick wall, so I can paint it. Know what I mean?"

I just nodded this time because he didn't really wait for a "sure."

"Things'll be different there. They have to be."

"They will be," I said.

"You really think so?"

"Sure."

"Thanks, Charlie."

That's kind of how it went all day. We went to see a movie. And we ate pizza. And every time Patrick started getting tired, we got coffee, and he ate another Mini Thin or two. When things started turning dusk outside, he showed me all the places he and Brad would meet. He didn't say much about them. He just stared.

We ended up at the golf course.

We sat on the eighteenth green, which was pretty high on a hill, and we watched the sun disappear. By this point, Patrick had bought a bottle of red wine with his fake ID, and we passed it back and forth. Just talking.

"Did you hear about Lily?" he asked.

"Who?"

"Lily Miller. I don't know what her real first name was, but they called her Lily. She was a senior when I was a sophomore."

"I don't think so."

"I thought your brother would have told you. It's a classic."

"Maybe."

"Okay. Stop me if you heard it."

"Okay."

"So, Lily comes up here with this guy who was the lead in all the plays."

"Parker?"

"Right, Parker. How did you know?"

"My sister had a crush on him."

"Perfect!" We were getting pretty drunk. "So, Parker and Lily come up here one night. And they are so in love! He even gave her his thespian pin or something."

At this point, Patrick is spitting out wine between sentences, he's laughing so hard.

"They even had a song. Something like *Broken Wings* by that band, Mr. Mister. I don't even know, but I hope it was *Broken Wings* because it would make the story perfect."

"Keep going," I encouraged.

"Okay. Okay." He swallowed. "So, they've been going out for a long time, and I think they've even had sex before, but this was going to be a special night. She packed a little picnic, and he brought a boom box to play *Broken Wings*."

Patrick just couldn't get over that song. He laughed for ten minutes.

"Okay. Okay. I'm sorry. So, they have this picnic with sandwiches and everything. They start to make out. The stereo's playing, and they're just about to 'do it' when Parker realizes he forgot the condoms. They're both naked on this putting green. They both want each other. There's no condom. So, what do you think happened?"

"I don't know."

"They did it doggie-style with one of the sandwich bags!"

"NO!" was all I could really say.

"YES!" was Patrick's rebuttal.

"GOD!" was my counter.

"YES!" was Patrick's conclusion.

After we shook off the giggles and wasted most of the wine with spit takes, he turned to me.

"And you want to know the best part?"

"What?"

"She was the valedictorian. And everyone knew it when she went up to give her speech!"

There's nothing like the deep breaths after laughing that hard. Nothing in the world like a sore stomach for the right reasons. It was that great.

So, Patrick and I shared all the stories we could think of.

▷ **12** *dusk:* Dämmerung **15** *green* (n): area of grass cut short around a hole in a golf course **17** *fake ID:* gefälschter Personalausweis **28** *lead* (n): main actor **32** *have a crush on sb.:* have strong feelings for sb. **35** *thespian pin:* badge which is given to a high-school student who has acted in several plays **39** *Mr. Mister:* pop band (1982–1989) **45** *boom box* (AE infml): large portable radio and tape player **51** *putting green* ['pʌtɪŋ]: small golf course for practising **56, 57** *rebuttal, counter:* (here) reply that is the opposite of the statement before **63** *valedictorian:* (cf. p. 183)

There was a kid named Barry, who used to build kites in art class. Then, after school, he would attach firecrackers to the kite and fly it and blow it up. He's now studying to be an air traffic controller.

—Patrick's story via Sam

And then there was this kid named Chip who spent all of his money from allowance and Christmas and birthdays to buy bug killing equipment and he would go door to door asking if he could kill the bugs for free.

—my story via my sister

There was a guy named Carl Burns and everyone called him C.B. And one day C.B. got so drunk at a party that he tried to "fuck" the host's dog.

—Patrick's story

And there was this guy they called "Action Jack" because supposedly he was caught masturbating at a drunk party. And at every pep rally, the kids would clap and chant. Action Jack … clap clap clap … Action Jack!

—my story via my brother

There were other stories and other names. Second Base Stace, who had breasts in the fourth grade and let some of the boys feel them. Vincent, who took acid and tried to flush a sofa down the toilet. Sheila, who allegedly masturbated with a hot dog and had to go to the emergency room. The list went on and on.

By the end, all I could think was what these people must feel like when they go to their class reunions. I wonder if they're embarrassed, and I wonder if that's a small price to pay for being a legend.

After we sobered up a bit with coffee and Mini Thins, Patrick drove me home. The mix tape I made for him hit a bunch of winter songs. And Patrick turned to me.

"Thanks, Charlie."

"Sure."

"No. I mean in the cafeteria."

"Sure."

After that, it was quiet. He drove me home and pulled up in the driveway. We hugged good night, and when I was just about to let go, he held me a little tighter. And he moved his face to mine. And he kissed me. A real kiss. Then, he pulled away real slow.

"I'm sorry."

"No. That's okay."

"Really. I'm sorry."

"No, really. It was okay."

So, he said "thanks" and hugged me again. And moved in to kiss me again. And I just let him. I don't know why. We stayed in his car for a long time.

We didn't do anything other than kiss. And we didn't even do that for very long. After a while, his eyes lost the glazey numb look from the wine or the coffee or the fact that he had stayed up the night before. Then, he started crying. Then, he started talking about Brad.

And I just let him. Because that's what friends are for.

Love always,
Charlie

May 17, 1992

Dear friend,

It seems like every morning since that first night, I wake up dull, and my head hurts, and I can't breathe. Patrick and I have been spending a lot of time together. We drink a lot. Actually, it's more like Patrick drinks, and I sip.

It's just hard to see a friend hurt this much. Especially when you can't do anything except "be there." I want to make him stop hurting, but I can't. So, I just follow him around whenever he wants to show me his world.

One night Patrick took me to this park where men go to find each other. Patrick told me that if I didn't want to be bothered by anyone that I should just not make eye contact. He said that eye contact is

▷ **1** *kite:* Drachen **6** *bug:* Ungeziefer **16** *pep rally* (AE): meeting held before a match to get spectators excited **25** *class reunion:* (cf. p. 181) **28** *hit sth.* (sl): (here) start playing sth. **54** *dull:* without energy **57** *sip:* drink sth., taking a very small amount each time

how you agree to fool around anonymously. Nobody talks. They just find places to go. After a while, Patrick saw someone he liked. He asked me if I needed any cigarettes, and when I said no, he patted my shoulder and walked away with this boy.

I just sat on a bench, looking around. All I saw were the shadows of people. Some on the ground. Some by a tree. Some just walking. It was so quiet. After a few minutes, I lit a cigarette, and I heard somebody whisper.

"You got an extra cigarette?" the voice asked.

I turned around and saw a man in shadow.

"Sure," I said.

I reached out to hand the man a cigarette. He took it.

"You got a light?" he said.

"Sure," I said, and I struck a match for him.

Instead of just leaning down and lighting the cigarette, he reached out to make a cup around the match with our hands, which is something we all do when it's windy. But it wasn't windy. I think he just wanted to touch my hands because while he was lighting the cigarette, he did it for a lot longer than necessary. Maybe he wanted me to see his face over the glow of the match. To see how handsome he was. I don't know. He did look familiar. But I couldn't figure out from where.

He blew out the match. "Thanks." And exhaled.

"No problem," I said.

"Mind if I sit down?" he asked.

"Not really."

He sat down. And said a few things. And it was his voice. I recognized his voice. So, I lit another cigarette and looked at his face again, and thought hard, and that's when I figured it out. It was the guy who does the sports on the TV news!

"Nice night," he said.

I couldn't believe it! I guess I managed to nod because he kept talking. About sports! He kept talking about how the designated hitter in baseball was bad and why basketball was a commercial success and what teams looked promising in college football. He even mentioned my brother's name! I swear!

All I said was, "So, what's it like being on television?"

It must have been the wrong thing to say because he just got up and walked away. It was too bad because I wanted to ask him if he thought my brother would make it to the pros.

Another night, Patrick took me to this place where they sell poppers, which is this drug you inhale. They didn't have poppers, but the guy behind the counter said that he had something that was just as good. So, Patrick bought that. It was in this aerosal can. We both took a sniff of it, and I swear we both thought we were going to die of a heart attack.

All in all, I think Patrick took me to about every place there is to go that I wouldn't have known about otherwise. There was this karaoke bar on one of the main streets in the city. And there was this dance club. And this one bathroom in this one gym. All these places. Sometimes, Patrick would pick up guys. Sometimes, he wouldn't. He said that it was hard being safe. And you never know.

The nights he would pick up someone always made him sad. It's hard, too, because Patrick began every night really excited. He always said he felt free. And tonight was his destiny. And things like that. But by the end of that night, he just looked sad. Sometimes, he would talk about Brad. Sometimes, he wouldn't. But after a while, the whole thing just wasn't interesting to him anymore, and he ran out of things to keep himself numb.

So, tonight, he dropped me off at home. It was the night we went back to the park where men meet. And the night he saw Brad there with some guy. Brad was too into what he was doing to notice us. Patrick didn't say anything. He didn't do anything. He just walked back to the car. And we drove in silence. On the way, he threw the bottle of wine out the window. And it landed with a crash. And this time he didn't try to kiss me like he had every night. He just thanked me for being his friend. And drove away.

Love always,
Charlie

▷ **33–34** *designated hitter:* one of the players in a baseball game **44** *aerosal* (usu. *aerosol*) *can:* Sprühdose **52** *be safe:* (here) have safer sex

May 21, 1992

Dear friend,

The school year is just about over. We have another month or so to go. But the seniors like my sister and Sam and Patrick only have a couple of weeks. Then, they have prom and graduation, and they are all busy making plans.

Mary Elizabeth is taking her new boyfriend, Peter. My sister is taking Erik. Patrick is going with Alice. And Craig agreed to go with Sam this time. They have even rented a limo and everything. Not my sister, though. She's going in her new boyfriend's car, which is a Buick.

Bill has been very sentimental lately because he can feel his first year of teaching coming to an end. At least that's what he said to me. He was planning on moving to New York and writing plays, but he told me that he doesn't really think he wants to anymore. He really likes teaching kids English and thinks maybe he can take over the drama department, too, next year.

I guess he's been thinking about this a lot because he hadn't given me a new book to read since *The Stranger*. He did ask me to watch a lot of movies, though, and write an essay about what I thought of all those movies. The movies were *The Graduate*, *Harold & Maude*, *My Life as a Dog* (which has subtitles!), *Dead Poets Society*, and a movie called *The Unbelievable Truth*, which was very hard to find.

I watched all the movies in one day. It was quite great.

The essay I wrote was very similar to the past few essays I wrote because everything Bill tells me to read or see are similar. Except the time he had me read *Naked Lunch*.

Incidentally, he told me he had given me that book because he had just broken up with his girlfriend and was feeling philosophical. I guess that's why he was sad that afternoon when we talked about *On the Road*. He apologized for letting his personal life affect his teaching, and I accepted because I didn't know what else to do. It's strange to think about your teachers as being people even when they're Bill. I guess he has since made up with his girlfriend. They're living together now. At least that's what he said.

So, in school Bill gave me my final book to read for the year. It's called *The Fountainhead*, and it's very long.

When he gave me the book, Bill said, "Be skeptical about this one. It's a great book. But try to be a filter, not a sponge."

Sometimes, I think Bill forgets that I am sixteen. But I am very happy that he does.

I haven't started reading it because I am very behind in my other classes because I spent so much time with Patrick. But if I can catch up, I will end my first year with straight A's, which makes me very happy. I almost didn't get an A in math, but then Mr. Carlo told me to stop asking "why?" all the time and just follow the formulas. So, I did. Now, I get perfect scores on all my tests. I just wish I knew what the formulas did. I honestly have no idea.

I was just thinking that I wrote to you first because I was afraid about starting high school. Today, I feel good, so that's kind of funny.

By the way, Patrick stopped drinking that night he saw Brad in the park. I guess he's feeling better. He just wants to graduate and go to college now.

I saw Brad in detention the Monday after I saw him at the park. And he looked just like he always looks.

Love always,
Charlie

May 27, 1992

Dear friend,

I've been reading *The Fountainhead* for the past few days, and it's an excellent book. I read on the back cover that the author was born in Russia and came to America when she was young. She barely spoke English, but she wanted to be a great writer. I thought that was very admirable, so I sat down and tried to write a story.

"Ian MacArthur is a wonderful sweet fellow who wears glasses and peers out of them with delight."

▷ **5** *prom:* (cf. p. 183) • *graduation:* (cf. p. 182) **9** *limo* ['lɪmoʊ] (infml): (Luxus)limousine **11** *Buick* ['bjuːɪk] **37** *"The Fountainhead":* novel (1943) by Ayn Rand (1905–1982) which celebrates human individualism **39** *sponge* [spʌndʒ]: Schwamm

That was the first sentence. The problem was that I just couldn't think of the next one. After cleaning my room three times, I decided to leave Ian alone for a while because I was starting to get mad at him.

I've had a lot of time to write and read and think about things this past week because everyone is busy with prom and graduation and schedules. Next Friday is their last day of school. And then prom is on Tuesday, which I thought was strange because I thought it would be on a weekend, but Sam told me that every school can't have their prom on the same night or else there wouldn't be enough tuxedos and restaurants to go around. I said it felt very well planned. And then Sunday is their graduation. It all feels very exciting. I wish it were happening to me.

I wonder what it will be like when I leave this place. The fact that I will have to have a roommate and buy shampoo. I thought how great it would be to go to my senior prom three years from now with Sam. I hope it's on a Friday. And I hope I will be a valedictorian at graduation. I wonder what my speech would be. And if Bill would help me with it if he didn't go to New York and write plays. Or maybe he would even if he was in New York writing plays. I think that would be especially nice of him.

I don't know. *The Fountainhead* is a very good book. I hope I am being a filter.

Love always,
Charlie

June 2, 1992

Dear friend,

Did you have a senior prank? I'm guessing you probably did because my sister said it's a tradition at a lot of schools. This year, the prank was as follows: Some seniors filled the swimming pool with about six thousand packages of grape Kool-Aid. I have no idea who thinks of these things or why, except that the senior prank is supposed to signify the end of school. What this has to do with a grape pool is beyond me, but I was very happy not to have gym.

It's actually been a very exciting time because we've all been busy finishing up the year. This Friday is the last day of school for all of my friends and my sister. They've been talking about their prom nonstop. Even the people that think it's a "joke" like Mary Elizabeth can't stop talking about what a "joke" it is. It's all very fun to witness.

So, by this time, everyone has finally figured out which schools he or she is going to next year. Patrick is going to the University of Washington because he wants to be near the music there. He says he thinks he wants to work for a record company someday. Maybe be a publicist or a person who finds new bands. Sam finally made her decision to leave early for the summer program at the college of her choice. I love that expression. College of my choice. Safety school is another favorite.

The thing was that Sam got into two schools. The college of her choice and a safety school. She could have started at the safety school in the fall, but in order to go to the college of her choice, she had to do this special summer program just like my brother. That's right! The school is Penn State, which is so great because now I can visit my brother and Sam with one trip. I don't want to think about Sam leaving just yet, but I did wonder what would happen if she and my brother ever started dating, which is stupid because they are nothing alike, and Sam is in love with Craig. I have to stop doing this.

My sister is going to a "small liberal arts college back East" called Sarah Lawrence. She almost didn't get to go because it costs a lot of money, but then she got an academic scholarship through the Rotary Club or Moose Lodge or something like that, which I thought was very generous of them. My sister is going to be second in her class. I thought she might have been valedictorian, but she got a B when she was going through that tough time with her old boyfriend.

Mary Elizabeth is going to Berkeley. And Alice is going to study movies at New York University. I never even knew she liked movies, but I guess she does. She calls them "films."

▷ **6** *schedule* ['skedʒuːl; BE 'ʃedjuːl]: plan that lists all the things you have to do and says when you must do them **9–10** *enough sth. to go around:* enough of sth. for everybody **9** *tuxedo* [tʌk'siːdoʊ] (BE: *dinner jacket/suit*): Smoking **27** *prank:* trick that is played on sb. as a joke **30** *Kool-Aid* (brand name): soft drink that you make by mixing powder with water **56** *liberal arts college:* (cf. p. 182)

Incidentally, I finished *The Fountainhead*. It was a really great experience. It's strange to describe reading a book as a really great experience, but that's kind of how it felt. It was a different book from the others because it wasn't about being a kid. And it wasn't like *The Stranger* or *Naked Lunch* even though I think it was philosophical in a way. But it wasn't like you had to really search for the philosophy. It was pretty straightforward, I thought, and the great part is that I took what the author wrote about and put it in terms of my own life. Maybe that's what being a filter means. I'm not sure.

There was this one part where the main character, who is this architect, is sitting on a boat with his best friend, who is a newspaper tycoon. And the newspaper tycoon says that the architect is a very cold man. The architect replies that if the boat were sinking, and there was only room in the lifeboat for one person, he would gladly give up his life for the newspaper tycoon. And then he says something like this …

"I would die for you. But I won't live for you."

Something like that. I think the idea is that every person has to live for his or her own life and then make the choice to share it with other people. Maybe that is what makes people "participate." I'm not really certain. Because I don't know if I would mind living for Sam for a while. Then again, she wouldn't want me to, so maybe it's a lot friendlier than all that. I hope so anyway.

I told my psychiatrist about the book and Bill and about Sam and Patrick and all their colleges, but he just keeps asking me questions about when I was younger. The thing is I feel that I'm just repeating the same memories to him. I don't know. He says it's important. I guess we'll have to see.

I would write a little more today, but I have to learn my math formulas for the final on Thursday. Wish me luck!

Love always,
Charlie

June 5, 1992

Dear friend,

I wanted to tell you about us running. There was this beautiful sunset. And there was this hill. The hill up to the eighteenth green where Patrick and I spit wine from laughing. And just a few hours before, Sam and Patrick and everyone I love and know had their last day of high school ever. And I was happy because they were happy. My sister even let me hug her in the hallway. Congratulations was the word of the day. So, Sam and Patrick and I went to the Big Boy and smoked cigarettes. Then, we went walking, waiting for it to be time to go to *Rocky Horror*. And we were talking about things that seemed important at the time. And we were looking up that hill. And then Patrick started running after the sunset. And Sam immediately followed him. And I saw them in silhouette. Running after the sun. Then, I started running. And everything was as good as it could be.

That night, Patrick decided to play Frank 'N Furter one last time. He was so happy to put on the costume, and everyone was happy he decided to do it. It was quite moving actually. He gave the best show I ever saw him give. Maybe I was biased, but I don't care. It was the show I'll always remember. Especially his last song.

The song is called "I'm Going Home." In the movie, Tim Curry, who plays the character, cries during that song. But Patrick was smiling. And it felt just right.

I even persuaded my sister to come to the show with her boyfriend. I have been trying to get her to come since I started going, but she never would. But this time she did. And since she and her boyfriend never saw the show before, they were technically "virgins," which meant they would have to do all these embarrassing things before the show started to get "initiated." I decided not to tell my sister this, and she and her boyfriend had to go on stage and try to dance the *Time Warp*.

Whoever lost the dance contest had to pretend he or she was having sex with a large stuffed Gumby doll, so I quickly showed my

▷ **7** *straightforward:* easy to understand, not complicated **12** *tycoon* [taɪ'kuːn]: person who is successful in business or industry and has become rich and powerful **51** *biased* ['baɪəst]: voreingenommen **62–63** *time warp:* Zeitverzerrung; name of a song from *The Rocky Horror Picture Show* **65** *Gumby doll:* cartoon character made out of plasticine (= Knetgummi)

sister and her boyfriend how to dance the *Time Warp*, so they wouldn't lose the contest. It was fun watching my sister dance the *Time Warp* on stage, but I don't think I could have handled her pretending to have sex with a large stuffed Gumby.

I asked my sister if she wanted to come to Craig's for the party afterward, but she said that one of her friends was having a party, so she was going to that. That was okay with me because at least she came to the show. And before she left, she hugged me again. Two in one day! I really do love my sister. Especially when she's nice.

The party at Craig's was great. Craig and Peter bought champagne to congratulate all the people who were graduating. And we danced. And we talked. And I saw Mary Elizabeth kissing Peter and looking happy. And I saw Sam kissing Craig and looking happy. And I saw Patrick and Alice not even care that they weren't kissing anybody because they were too excited talking about their futures.

So, I just sat there with a bottle of champagne near the CD player, and I changed the songs to fit the mood of what I saw. I was lucky, too, because Craig has an excellent collection. When people looked a little tired, I played something fun. When they looked like they wanted to talk, I played something soft. It was a great way to sit alone at a party and still feel a part of things.

After the party, everyone thanked me because they said it was the perfect music. Craig said that I should be a deejay to make money while I was still in school just like he does modeling. I thought that was a good idea. Maybe I could save up a lot of money, so I would be able to go to college even if something like the Rotary Club or Moose Lodge didn't come through.

My brother said recently on the phone that if he makes it to the pros, I don't have to worry about my college money at all. He said he'd take care of it. I can't wait to see my brother. He's coming home for my sister's graduation, which is so nice.

Love always,
Charlie

June 9, 1992

Dear friend,

It is now prom night. And I am sitting in my room. Yesterday was difficult because I didn't know anybody since all my friends and my sister were no longer in school.

The worst was lunchtime because it reminded me of when everyone was angry with me for Mary Elizabeth. I couldn't even eat my sandwich, and my mom made my favorite because I think she knew how sad I would be with everyone gone.

The halls seemed different. And the juniors were acting different because they are now the seniors. They even had T-shirts made. I don't know who plans these things.

All I can think about is the fact that Sam is leaving in two weeks to go to Penn State. And Mary Elizabeth is going to be busy with her guy. And my sister is going to be busy with hers. And Alice and I aren't that close. I know Patrick will be around, but I'm afraid that maybe since he isn't sad, he won't want to spend time with me. I know that's wrong in my head, but it feels that way sometimes. So, then the only person I would have to talk to would be my psychiatrist, and I don't like the idea of that right now because he keeps asking me questions about when I was younger, and they're starting to get weird.

I'm just lucky that I have so much schoolwork and don't have a lot of time to think.

All I hope is that tonight is great for the people whom it's supposed to be great for. My sister's boyfriend showed up in his Buick, and he was wearing a white "tails" coat over a black suit, which looked wrong for some reason. His "cumberbunn" (I don't know how to spell this) matched my sister's dress, which was powder blue and low-cut. It reminded me of those magazines. I have to stop spinning out like this. Okay.

All I hope is that my sister feels beautiful, and her new guy makes her feel beautiful. I hope that Craig doesn't make Sam feel that her prom isn't special just because he's older. I hope the same for Mary Elizabeth with Peter. I hope Brad and Patrick decide to make up and

▷ **59** *white "tails":* weißer Frack **60** *cumberbunn* = *cummerbund* ['kʌmərbʌnd]: wide band of fabric worn around the waist, esp. with a tuxedo **61–62** *low-cut:* tief ausgeschnitten **62** *spin out:* (here) leave the main point of what you are saying

dance in front of the whole school. And that Alice is secretly a lesbian and in love with Brad's girlfriend Nancy (and vice versa), so nobody feels left out. I hope the deejay is as good as everyone said I was last Friday. And I hope everyone's pictures turn out great and never become old photographs and nobody gets in a car accident.

That is what I really hope.

Love always,
Charlie

June 10, 1992

Dear friend,

I just got home from school, and my sister is still asleep from the after-prom party the school organized. I called over to Patrick and Sam's, but they're still asleep, too. Patrick and Sam have a cordless phone which always runs out of batteries, and Sam's mom sounded like a mom in the *Peanuts* cartoons. Wah Wah … Wuh.

I had two finals today. One in biology, which I think I got a perfect in. The other in Bill's class. The final was about *The Great Gatsby*. The only thing hard about it was the fact that he had me read the book so long ago, and it was difficult to remember.

After I handed in the final, I asked Bill if he wanted me to write an essay about *The Fountainhead*, since I told him that I had finished it, and he hadn't told me to do anything. He said that it wouldn't be fair to have me write another essay when I have so many finals this week. Instead, he invited me over to his town house to spend Saturday afternoon with his girlfriend and him, which sounds like fun.

So, on Friday, I will go to *Rocky Horror*. Then, on Saturday, I will go over to Bill's town house. Then, on Sunday, I will watch everyone graduate and spend time with my brother and all the family because of my sister. Then, I'll probably go to Sam and Patrick's to celebrate their graduating. Then, I'll have two more days of school, which doesn't make sense because all my finals will be over. But they have some activities planned. At least that's what I've heard.

The reason I am thinking so far in advance is because school is terribly lonely. I think I've said that before, but it's getting harder every day. I have two finals tomorrow. History and typing. Then, on Friday, I have finals in all my other classes like gym and shop. I don't know if there will be actual finals in these classes. Especially shop. I think Mr. Callahan will just play some of his old records for us. He did that when we were supposed to have a midterm, too, but it won't be the same without Patrick lip-synching. Incidentally, I got a perfect on my math final last week.

Love always,
Charlie

June 13, 1992

Dear friend,

I just got home from Bill's house. I would have written to you about last night this morning, but I had to go to Bill's.

Last night, Craig and Sam broke up.

It was very sad to watch. In the past few days, I have heard a lot about the prom, and thanks to those twenty-four-hour film places, I have seen what everyone looked like. Sam looked beautiful. Patrick looked handsome. Mary Elizabeth, Alice, Mary Elizabeth's boyfriend all looked great, too. The only thing is that Alice wore white stick deodorant with a strapless dress, and it showed. I don't think that kind of thing matters, but supposedly Alice was paranoid about it all night. Craig looked handsome as well, but he wore a suit instead of a tux. That's not why they broke up.

Actually, the prom was supposed to be very nice. The limo was really great, and the limo driver got everyone stoned, which made the very expensive food taste even better. His name was Billy. The prom's music came from this really bad cover band called The Gypsies of the Allegheny, but the drummer was good, so everyone had a nice time

▷ **41** *lip-synch* ['lɪpsɪŋk]: move your mouth without singing, so that its movements match the sound on a recorded song

dancing. Patrick and Brad didn't even look at each other, but Sam said Patrick was really okay about it.

After the prom, my sister and her boyfriend went to the after-prom party the school organized. It was at this popular dance club downtown. She said that it was really fun with everyone all dressed up and dancing to good music played by a deejay instead of The Gypsies of the Allegheny. They even had a comedian who did impersonations. The only thing was that once you went in, you couldn't leave and come back. I guess the parents thought that it would keep the kids out of trouble. But nobody seemed to mind. They were having too much fun, and enough people smuggled in liquor anyway.

After the party, it was about seven o'clock in the morning and everyone went to the Big Boy for pancakes or bacon.

I asked Patrick how he liked the after-prom party, and he said that it was a lot of fun. He said that Craig had rented a hotel suite for all of them, but only Craig and Sam went. Actually, Sam wanted to go to the after-prom party the school organized, too, but Craig got really angry because he already paid for the hotel suite. That's not why they broke up.

It happened yesterday at Craig's house after *Rocky Horror*. Like I said, Mary Elizabeth's boyfriend, Peter, is good friends with Craig, and he kind of stepped into the middle of things. I guess he really likes Mary Elizabeth a lot and has grown to like Sam quite a bit because he's the one who brought it up. Nobody even suspected.

Basically, Craig had been cheating on Sam ever since they started going out. And when I say cheat, I don't mean he got drunk once and fooled around with one girl and felt bad about it. There were several girls. Several times. Drunk and sober. And I guess he never felt bad.

The reason Peter didn't say anything at first was the fact that he didn't know anybody. And he didn't know Sam. He just thought she was this dumb high school girl because that's what Craig always told him.

Anyway, after he got to know Sam, Peter kept telling Craig that Craig had to tell her the truth because she wasn't just some dumb high school girl. Craig kept promising he would, but he never did it. There was always some excuse. Craig called them "reasons."

"I don't want to ruin the prom for her."

"I don't want to ruin graduation for her."

"I don't want to ruin the show for her."

Then, finally, Craig said there was no point telling her anything at all. She was about to go away to college anyway. She would find a new guy. He was always "safe" about other girls. There was nothing to worry about in that way. And why not just let Sam remember the whole experience in a good way? Because he really liked Sam and didn't want to hurt her feelings.

Peter went along with this logic even though he thought it was wrong. At least that's what he said. But then after the show yesterday, Craig told him that he fooled around with yet another girl the afternoon of the prom. That's when Peter told Craig that if Craig didn't say something to Sam, he would. Well, Craig didn't say anything, and Peter still didn't think it was his business, but then he overheard Sam at the party. She was talking to Mary Elizabeth about how Craig might be "the one" and how she was trying to think of ways to keep it going long-distance while she was at school. Letters. Phone calls. Vacations. And breaks. That was it for Peter.

He went up to Craig and said, "You tell her something now, or I tell her everything."

So, Craig pulled Sam into his bedroom. They were in there for a while. Then, Sam walked from the bedroom straight out the front door, silently sobbing. Craig didn't run after her. That was probably the worst part. Not that he should have tried to get back together with her, but I think he should have run after her anyway.

All I know is that Sam was devastated. Mary Elizabeth and Alice went after her to make sure she was okay. I would have gone, too, but Patrick grabbed my arm to stay. He wanted to know what was going on, I guess, or maybe he figured Sam would be better off with female company.

I'm glad that we stayed, though, because I think our presence prevented a pretty violent fight between Craig and Peter. Because we were there, all they really did was scream at each other. That's where I heard most of the details I'm writing to you about.

Craig would say, "Fuck you, Peter! Fuck you!"

▷ **8** *impersonation:* imitation of a famous person **11** *liquor* ['lɪkər]: strong alcoholic drink **64** *devastated* ['devəsteɪtəd]: extremely upset and shocked

And Peter would say, “Don’t blame me that you fucked around on her since the beginning! The afternoon of her prom!? You’re just a bastard! You hear me?! A fucking bastard!”

Things like that.

When it looked like things were going to get violent, Patrick stepped between the two and, with my help, got Peter out of the apartment. When we got outside, the girls were gone. So, Patrick and I got into Patrick’s car and drove Peter home. He was still seething, so he “vented” about Craig. That’s where I heard the rest of the details I’m writing to you about. Finally, we dropped Peter off, and he made us promise to make sure Mary Elizabeth didn’t think he was cheating on her because he wasn’t. He just didn’t want to be found “guilty by association” with that “prick.”

We promised, and he went into his apartment building.

Patrick and I weren’t sure how much Craig actually told Sam. We both hoped he gave her a “soft” version of the truth. Enough to make her stay away. But not enough to make her doubt everything about everything. Maybe it’s better to know the whole truth. I honestly don’t know.

So, we just made a pact that we wouldn’t tell her unless we found out that Craig made it sound like “nothing big,” and Sam was ready to forgive him. I hope it doesn’t come to that. I hope Craig told her enough to make her stay away.

We drove around to all the places where we thought we might find the girls, but we couldn’t find them. Patrick figured they were probably just driving around, trying to let Sam “cool off a bit.”

So, Patrick dropped me at home. He said he’d call me tomorrow when he heard anything.

I remember going to sleep last night, and I realized something. Something that I think is important. I realized that throughout the course of the evening, I wasn’t happy about Craig and Sam breaking up. Not at all.

I never once thought that it would mean Sam might start liking me. All I cared about was the fact that Sam got really hurt. And I guess I realized at that moment that I really did love her. Because there was nothing to gain, and that didn’t matter.

It was hard walking up the steps to Bill’s town house that afternoon because I didn’t receive a phone call all morning from

Patrick. And I was so worried about Sam. I called on the phone, but nobody was there.

Bill looks different without a suit. He was wearing his old graduate school T-shirt. Which was Brown. The school. Not the color. His girlfriend was wearing sandals and a nice flowered dress. She even had hair under her arms. No kidding! They looked very happy together. And I was glad for Bill.

Their house didn't have a lot of furniture in it, but it was very comfortable. They had a lot of books, which I spent about a half an hour asking them about. There was also a picture of Bill and his girlfriend when they were at Brown together in graduate school. Bill had very long hair then.

Bill's girlfriend made lunch while Bill made the salad. I just sat in the kitchen, drinking a ginger ale, and watching them. The lunch was a spaghetti dish of some sort because Bill's girlfriend doesn't eat meat. Bill doesn't eat meat either now. The salad did have imitation bacon bits, though, because bacon is the only thing they both miss.

They had a really nice collection of jazz records, and they kept playing them all through lunch. After a while, they broke open a bottle of white wine and gave me another ginger ale. Then, we started talking.

Bill asked me about *The Fountainhead*, and I told him, making sure that I was a filter.

Then, he asked me about how I liked my first year of high school, and I told him, making sure that I included all the stories in which I "participated."

Then, he asked me about girls, and I told him how I really loved Sam, and how I wondered what the lady who wrote *The Fountainhead* would say about how I came to realize that I loved her.

After I finished, Bill got very quiet. He cleared his throat.

"Charlie ... I want to thank you."

"Why?" I said.

"Because it has been a wonderful experience teaching you."

"Oh ... I'm glad." I didn't know what else to say.

▷ **8** *seethe:* be extremely angry about sth. without shouting, etc. **9** *vent about sb./sth.:* express feelings, esp. anger, strongly about sb./sth. **13** *prick* (sl): terrible person **44** *have hair under her arms:* (this is usu. considered taboo in the USA)

Then, Bill took this really long pause, and his voice sounded like my dad when he wants to have a big talk.

"Charlie," he said. "Do you know why I gave you all that extra work?"

I shook my head no. That look on his face. It made me quiet.

"Charlie, do you know how smart you are?"

I just shook my head no again. He was talking for real. It was strange.

"Charlie, you're one of the most gifted people I've ever known. And I don't mean in terms of my other students. I mean in terms of anyone I've ever met. That's why I gave you the extra work. I was wondering if you were aware of that?"

"I guess so. I don't know." I felt really strange. I didn't know where this was coming from. I just wrote some essays.

"Charlie. Please don't take this the wrong way. I'm not trying to make you feel uncomfortable. I just want you to know that you're very special … and the only reason I'm telling you is that I don't know if anyone else ever has."

I looked up at him. And then I didn't feel strange. I felt like I wanted to cry. He was being so nice to me, and the way his girlfriend looked, I knew that this meant a lot to him. And I didn't know why it did.

"So, when the school year ends, and I'm not your teacher anymore, I want you to know that if you ever need anything, or want to know about more books, or want to show me anything you write, or anything, you can always come to me as a friend. I do consider you a friend, Charlie."

I started crying a little bit. I actually think his girlfriend was, too. But Bill wasn't. He looked very solid. I just remember wanting to hug him. But I've never done that before, and I guess Patrick and girls and family don't count. I didn't say anything for a while because I didn't know what to say.

So, finally I just said, "You're the best teacher I ever had."

And he said, "Thank you."

And that was that. Bill didn't try to make sure that I would see him next year if I needed anything. He didn't ask me why I was crying. He just let me hear what he had to say in my own way and let things be. That was probably the best part.

After a few minutes, it was time for me to leave. I don't know who decides these things. It just happens.

So, we went to the door, and Bill's girlfriend hugged me good-bye, which was very nice considering I didn't know her except for today. Then, Bill extended his hand, and I took it. And we shook hands. And I even sneaked in a quick hug before I said "good-bye."

When I was driving home, I just thought about the word "special." And I thought the last person who said that about me was my aunt Helen. I was very grateful to have heard it again. Because I guess we all forget sometimes. And I think everyone is special in their own way. I really do.

My brother gets home tonight. And everyone's graduation is tomorrow. Patrick still hasn't called. I called him, but no one was home again. So, I decided to go out and buy everyone their graduation presents. I really haven't had time to do that until now.

Love always,
Charlie

June 16, 1992

Dear friend,

I just rode home on the bus. It was the last day of school for me today. And it was raining. When I do ride the bus, I usually sit toward the middle because I've heard sitting in the front is for nerds and sitting in the back is for squids, and the whole thing makes me nervous. I don't know what they call "squids" in other schools.

Anyway, today I decided to sit in the front with my legs over the whole seat. Kind of like I was lying down with my back to the window. I did this so I could look back at the other kids on the bus. I'm glad school buses don't have seat belts, or else I wouldn't have been able to do it.

▷ **9** *gifted:* having a lot of natural ability or intelligence **44** *sneak sth. in:* do sth. quickly **60** *nerd* (sl): person who is boring and unfashionable **61** *squid* (AE sl): student who studies a lot

The one thing I noticed was how different everyone looked. When we were all little, we used to sing songs on the bus ride home from the last day of school. The favorite song was a Pink Floyd song, I found out later, called *Another Brick in the Wall, Part II*. But there was this other song we loved even more because it ended with a swear. It went like this …

No more pencils / no more books / no more teachers' dirty looks / when the teacher rings the bell / drop your books and run like hell.

When we finished, we looked at the bus driver for a tense second. Then, we all laughed because we knew we could get in trouble for swearing, but the strength of our numbers would prevent any retribution. We were too young to know that the bus driver didn't care about our song. That all he wanted to do was go home after work. And maybe sleep off the drinks he had at lunch. Back then, it didn't matter. The nerds and the squids were one.

My brother came home Saturday night. And he looked even more different than the kids on the school bus looked compared to the beginning of the year. He had a beard! I was so happy! He also smiled different and was more "courteous." We all sat down to dinner, and everyone asked him questions about college. Dad asked about football. Mom asked about classes. I asked for all the fun stories. My sister asked nervous questions about what college is "really" like and would she put on the "freshman fifteen"? I don't know what this is, but I'm guessing it means you get fatter.

I was expecting my brother to just talk and talk about himself for a long time. He would do that whenever there was a big game in high school or the prom or something. But he seemed a lot more interested in what we were all doing, especially my sister with her graduation.

So, while they were talking, I suddenly remembered the TV news sports man and what he said about my brother. I got so excited. And I told my whole family. And this is what happened as a result.

My dad said, "Hey! How about that?!"

My brother said, "Really!?"

I said, "Yeah. I talked to him."

My brother said, "Did he say something good?"

My father said, "Any press is good press." I don't know where my father learns these things.

My brother kept going. "What did he say?"

I said, "Well, I think he said that college sports puts a lot of pressure on the students who do them." My brother kept nodding. "But he said that it built character. And he said that Penn State was looking really good with their recruitment. And he mentioned you."

My dad said, "Hey! How about that?"

My brother said, "Really?"

I said, "Yeah. I talked to him."

My brother said, "When did you talk to him?"

I said, "A couple weeks ago."

And then I froze because I suddenly remembered the other part. The fact that I met the man in the park at night. And the fact that I gave him one of my cigarettes. And the fact that he was trying to pick me up. I just sat there, hoping it would go away. But it didn't.

"Where did you meet him, honey?" my mom asked.

The room turned pins and needles quiet. And I did my best impersonation of myself when I can't remember something. And here's what's going on inside my head.

Okay ... he came to school to have a talk with the class ... no ... my sister would know it was a lie ... I met him at the Big Boy ... he was with his family ... no ... my dad would scold me for bothering the "poor man" ... he said it on a news cast ... but I said I talked to him ... wait ...

"In the park. I was there with Patrick," I said.

My dad said, "Was he there with his family? Did you bother the poor man?"

"No. He was alone."

That was enough for my dad and everybody else, and I didn't even have to lie. Luckily, the attention was turned off me when my mother said what she likes to say when we're all together celebrating something.

"Who's in the mood for ice cream?"

▷ **5** *swear* [swer] (n) (usu. *swear word*): (here) rude or taboo word **13** *retribution:* punishment **20** *courteous* ['kɜːrtiəs]: polite and well-behaved **54** *pins and needles quiet:* (here) so quiet that you could here a pin or a needle drop **59** *scold sb.:* speak angrily to sb. because he or she has done sth. wrong

Everyone was except for my sister. I think she was worried about the "freshman fifteen."

The next morning started early. I still hadn't heard from Patrick or Sam or anybody, but I knew I would see them at graduation, so I tried not to worry too much. All my relatives, including my dad's family from Ohio, came to the house around ten A.M. The two families really don't like each other, except for all us younger cousins because we don't know any better.

We had this big brunch with champagne, and just like last year for my brother's graduation, my mom gave her dad (my grandfather) sparkling apple juice instead of champagne because she didn't want him to get drunk and make a scene. And he said the same thing he said last year.

"This is good champagne."

I don't think he knew the difference because he's a beer drinker. Sometimes, whiskey.

Around twelve-thirty, brunch was over. All the cousins drove all the cars because the adults were still a little too drunk to drive to the graduation. Except for my dad, because he was too busy videotaping everyone with a camera he rented from the video store.

"Why buy a camera when you only need it three times a year?"

So, my sister, brother, dad, mom, and I each had to go in a different car to make sure nobody got lost. I went with all my Ohio cousins, who promptly pulled out a "joint" and passed it around. I didn't smoke any of it because I wasn't in the mood, and they said what they always say.

"Charlie, you're such a pussy."

So, all the cars pulled into the parking lot, and we all got out. And my sister yelled at my cousin Mike for rolling down the window while he was driving and messing up her hair.

"I was smoking a cigarette," was his reply.

"Couldn't you wait ten minutes?" was my sister's.

"But it was a great song," was his final word.

So, as my dad was getting the video camera out of the trunk, and my brother was talking to some of the graduating girls who were a year older and "looking good," my sister went for my mom to get my mom's purse. The great thing about my mom's purse is that no matter what you need at any given moment, she has it. When I was little, I used to call it the "first-aid kit" because that's all we needed back then. I still can't figure out how she does it.

After primping, my sister followed the trail of graduation caps to the field, and we all found our way to the bleachers. I sat in between my mom and brother since my dad was off getting a better camera angle. And my mom kept shushing my grandfather, who kept talking about how many black people were in the school.

When she couldn't stop him, she mentioned my story about the TV news sports man talking about my brother. This made my grandfather call my brother over to talk about it. This was smart on my mom's part because my brother is the only person who can get my grandfather to stop making a scene because he's really direct about it. After the story, this is what happened ...

"Jesus. Look at these bleachers. How many colored people—" My brother cut him off.

"Okay, Grandpa. Here's the deal. If you embarrass us one more time, I'm going to drive you back to the nursing home, and you'll never see your granddaughter give a speech." My brother is real tough.

"But then you won't see the speech either, big shot." My grandfather's real tough, too.

"Yeah, but my dad is videotaping it. And I can arrange it so I get to see the tape, and you don't. Can't I?"

My grandfather has a really weird smile. Especially when someone else wins. He didn't say anything more about it. He just started talking about football and didn't even mention anything about my brother playing on a team with black kids. I can't tell you how bad it was last year since my brother was on the field graduating instead of up in the bleachers making my grandfather stop.

While they were talking football, I kept looking for Patrick and Sam, but all I saw were those graduation caps in the distance. When the music started, the caps started marching toward the folding chairs set up on the field. That's when I finally saw Sam walking behind Patrick. I was so relieved. I couldn't really tell if she was happy or sad, but it was enough just to see her and know that she was there.

▷ **27** *pussy* (sl): weak or cowardly person **37** *purse* (AE): handbag **39** *first-aid kit:* Erste-Hilfe-Ausrüstung **41** *primp* (derog): make up your face • *graduation cap:* (cf. p. 182) **57** *big shot* (infml): clever person

When all the kids got in the chairs, the music stopped. And Mr. Small got up and gave a speech about what a wonderful class this was. He mentioned some of the achievements the school had made, and he emphasized how much they needed support at the Community Day Bake Sale to start a new computer lab. Then, he introduced the class president, who gave a speech. I don't know what class presidents do, but the girl gave a very good speech.

Then, it was time for the five top honor students to give a speech. That's the tradition in the school. My sister was second in her class, so she gave the fourth speech. The valedictorian is always last. Then, Mr. Small and the vice principal, whom Patrick swears is gay, hand out the diplomas.

The first three speeches were very similar. They all had quotes from pop songs that had something to do with the future. And all through the speeches, I could see my mother's hands. She was gripping them tighter and tighter together.

When they announced my sister's name, my mom uncoiled into applause. It was really great watching my sister get on the podium because my brother was something like 223rd in his class and consequently didn't get to give a speech. And maybe I'm biased, but when my sister quoted a pop song and talked about the future, it seemed great. I looked over at my brother, and he looked over at me. And we both smiled. Then, we looked at my mother, and she was crying real soft and messy, so my brother and I each took one of her hands. She looked at us and smiled and cried harder. Then, we both rested our heads on her shoulders, like a sideways hug, which made her cry even harder. Or maybe it let her cry even harder. I'm not sure which. But she gave our hands a little squeeze and said, "My boys," real soft, and went back to crying. I love my mom so much. I don't care if that's corny to say. I think on my next birthday, I'm going to buy her a present. I think that should be the tradition. The kid gets gifts from everybody, and he buys one present for his mom since she was there, too. I think that would be nice.

When my sister finished her speech, we all clapped and yelled, but nobody clapped or yelled louder than my grandfather. Nobody.

I don't remember what the valedictorian said except that she quoted Henry David Thoreau instead of a pop song.

Then, Mr. Small got up on the stage and asked everyone to refrain from applause until all the names were read and all the diplomas were handed out. I should mention that this didn't work last year either.

So, I saw my sister get her diploma and my mother cry again. And then I saw Mary Elizabeth. And I saw Alice. And I saw Patrick. And I saw Sam. It was a great day. Even when I saw Brad. It seemed okay.

We all met my sister in the parking lot, and the first one to hug her was my grandfather. He really is a proud man in his way. Everyone said how much they loved my sister's speech even if they didn't. Then, we all saw my father walking across the parking lot, holding the video camera above his head triumphantly. I don't think anybody hugged my sister longer than my dad. I looked around for Sam and Patrick, but I couldn't find them anywhere.

On the way home for the party, my Ohio cousins lit up another joint. This time, I took a hit, but they still called me a "pussy." I don't know why. Maybe that's just what Ohio cousins do. That and tell jokes.

"What has 32 legs and 1 tooth?"

"What?" we all asked.

"A West Virginia unemployment line."

Things like that.

When we got home, my Ohio cousins went straight for the bar because graduations seem to be the one occasion where anyone can drink. At least it was like that last year and this year. I wonder what my graduation will be like. It seems very far away.

So, my sister spent the first hour of the party opening up all the gifts, and her smile grew with each check, sweater, or fifty dollar bill. Nobody in our family is rich, but it seems like everybody saves up just enough for these kind of events, and we all pretend we're rich for a day.

The only people who didn't get my sister money or a sweater were my brother and I. My brother promised to take her out one day to shop for college things like soap, which he would pay for, and I bought her a little house that was hand-carved out of stone and painted in England. I told her I wanted to give her something that

▷ **17** *uncoil:* straighten out **30** *corny* (infml): too sentimental **38–39** *refrain from (doing) sth.:* not do sth.

makes her feel like she's at home even after she goes away. My sister actually kissed my cheek for that.

But the best part of the party happened when my mother came to me and said I had a phone call. I went to the phone.

"Hello?"

"Charlie?"

"Sam!"

"When are you coming over?" she asked.

"Now!" I said.

Then, my father, who was drinking a whiskey sour, growled, "You're not going anywhere until your relatives leave. You hear me?"

"Uh, Sam ... I have to wait for my relatives to leave," I said.

"Okay ... we'll be here until seven. Then, we'll call you from wherever we are." Sam really sounded happy.

"Okay, Sam. Congratulations!"

"Thanks, Charlie. Bye."

"Bye."

I hung up the phone.

I swear to you, I thought my relatives would never leave. Every story they told. Every pig in a blanket they ate. Every photograph they looked at, and every time I heard "when you were this high" with the appropriate gesture. It was like the clock stopped. It's not that I minded the stories because I didn't. And the pigs in blankets were quite good. But I wanted to see Sam.

At about 9:30, everyone was stuffed and sober. At 9:45, the hugs were over. At 9:50, the driveway was clear. My father gave me twenty dollars and the keys to his car, saying, "Thanks for sticking around. It meant a lot to me and the family." He was tipsy, but meant it just the same. Sam had told me they were going to a dance club downtown. So, I loaded everyone's gifts in my trunk, climbed in the car, and drove away.

There's something about that tunnel that leads to downtown. It's glorious at night. Just glorious. You start on one side of the mountain, and it's dark, and the radio is loud. As you enter the tunnel, the wind gets sucked away, and you squint from the lights overhead. When you adjust to the lights, you can see the other side in the distance just as the sound of the radio fades to nothing because the waves just can't reach. Then, you're in the middle of the tunnel, and everything becomes a calm dream. As you see the opening get closer, you just can't get there fast enough. And finally, just when you think you'll never get there, you see the opening right in front of you. And the radio comes back even louder than you remember it. And the wind is waiting. And you fly out of the tunnel onto the bridge. And there it is. The city. A million lights and buildings and everything seems as exciting as the first time you saw it. It really is a grand entrance.

After about half an hour looking around the dance club, I finally saw Mary Elizabeth with Peter. They were both drinking scotch and sodas, which Peter bought since he is older and had his hand stamped. I congratulated Mary Elizabeth and asked where everybody was. She told me that Alice was getting high in the ladies' room and Sam and Patrick were on the floor dancing. She said to just have a seat until they come back because she didn't know where they were specifically. So, I sat down and listened to Peter argue with Mary Elizabeth about the Democratic candidates. Again, the clock seemed to stop. I wanted to see Sam that badly.

After about three songs, Sam and Patrick came back completely coated in sweat.

"Charlie!"

I stood up, and we all hugged like we hadn't seen each other in months. Considering everything that happened, I guess that makes sense. After we let go, Patrick lay on top of Peter and Mary Elizabeth like they were a sofa. Then, he took Mary Elizabeth's drink out of her hand and drank it. "Hey, asshole" was her response. I think he was drunk, even though he hasn't been drinking lately, but Patrick does that stuff sober, so it's hard to tell.

That's when Sam grabbed my hand. "I love this song!"

She led me to the dance floor. And she started dancing. And I started dancing. It was a fast song, so I wasn't very good, but she didn't seem to mind. We were just dancing, and that was enough. The song ended, and then a slow one came on. She looked at me. I looked at her. Then, she took my hands and pulled me in to dance slow. I don't know how to dance slow very well either, but I do know how to sway.

▷ **10** *whiskey sour:* drink made of whiskey and lemon juice **20** *pig in a blanket:* type of party food usu. made of a sausage in pastry **21** *high:* (here) tall **25** *stuffed* (infml): full of food • *sober:* no longer under the influence of drink **28** *tipsy* (infml): slightly drunk **73** *sway:* move your body from side to side

Her whisper smelled like cranberry juice and vodka.

"I looked for you in the parking lot today."

I hoped mine still smelled like toothpaste.

"I was looking for you, too."

Then, we were quiet for the rest of the song. She held me a little closer. I held her a little closer. And we kept dancing. It was the one time all day that I really wanted the clock to stop. And just be there for a long time.

After the dance club, we went back to Peter's apartment, and I gave everyone their graduation presents. I gave Alice a film book about *Night of the Living Dead*, which she liked, and I gave Mary Elizabeth a copy of *My Life as a Dog* on videotape with the subtitles in it, which she loved.

Then, I gave Patrick and Sam their presents. I even wrapped them up special. I used the Sunday funny papers because they are in color. Patrick tore through his. Sam didn't rip any of the paper. She just plucked off the tape. And they looked at what was inside each box.

I gave Patrick *On the Road, Naked Lunch, The Stranger, This Side of Paradise, Peter Pan*, and *A Separate Peace*.

I gave Sam *To Kill a Mockingbird, The Catcher in the Rye, The Great Gatsby, Hamlet, Walden*, and *The Fountainhead.*

Under the books was a card that I wrote using the typewriter Sam bought me. The cards said that these were my copies of all my favorite books, and I wanted Sam and Patrick to have them because they were my two favorite people in the whole world.

When they both looked up from reading, they were quiet. Nobody smiled or cried or did anything. We were just open, looking at each other. They knew I meant the cards I wrote. And I knew it meant a lot to them.

"What do the cards say?" Mary Elizabeth asked.

"Do you mind, Charlie?" Patrick asked.

I shook my head no, and they each read their cards while I went to fill up my coffee cup with red wine.

When I came back, they all looked at me, and I said, "I'm going to miss you all very much. I hope you have a great time at college." And then I started crying because it suddenly hit me that they were all leaving. I think Peter thinks I'm a little strange. So, Sam stood up and took me into the kitchen, telling me on the way there that it was "okay." When we got to the kitchen, I was a little more calm.

Sam said, "You know I'm leaving in a week, Charlie?"

"Yeah. I know."

"Don't start crying again."

"Okay."

"I want you to listen."

"Okay."

"I'm really scared to be alone at college."

"You are?" I asked. I never really thought of that before.

"Just like you're really scared to be alone here."

"Okay." I nodded.

"So, I'll make you a deal. When things get to be too much at college, I'll call you, and when things get to be too much here, you call me."

"Could we write letters back and forth?"

"Of course," she said.

Then, I started crying again. I really am a roller-coaster sometimes. But Sam was patient.

"Charlie, I'm going to be back at the end of the summer, but before we think about that, let's just enjoy this last week together. All of us. Okay?"

I nodded and calmed down.

We spent the rest of the night just drinking and listening to music like we always did, but this time it was at Peter's, and it was better than Craig's, actually, because Peter has a better music collection. It was about one o'clock in the morning when it suddenly occurred to me.

"Oh my God!" I said.

"What's wrong, Charlie?"

"Tomorrow's a school day!"

I don't think I could have made them laugh harder.

Peter took me into the kitchen to make coffee, so I could sober up to drive home. I had about eight cups in a row and was ready to drive in about twenty minutes. The problem was, by the time I got home, I was so awake from the coffee, I couldn't fall asleep. By the time I got to school, I felt like dying. Luckily, all the finals were over, and all we did all day was watch film strips. I don't think I ever slept better. I was glad, too, because school really is lonely without them.

▷ **55** *roller-coaster:* Achterbahn

Today was different because I didn't sleep, and I didn't get to see Sam or Patrick last night because they were having a special dinner out with their parents. And my brother was on a date with one of the girls who was "looking good" at graduation. My sister was busy with her boyfriend. And my mom and dad were still tired from the graduation party.

Today, pretty much every teacher just let the kids sit around and talk after we handed in our textbooks. I honestly didn't know anybody, except maybe for Susan, but after that time in the hallway, she's avoided me more than ever. So, I didn't really talk. The only good class was Bill's because I got to talk to Bill. It was hard saying good-bye to him after class was over, but he said that it wasn't good-bye. I could call him anytime over the summer if I wanted to talk or borrow books, and that made me feel a little better.

This one kid with crooked teeth named Leonard called me a "teacher's pet" in the hallway after Bill's class, but I didn't mind because I think he missed the point somewhere.

I ate lunch outside on a bench where we all used to smoke. After I ate my Ho-Ho, I lit up a cigarette, and I was kind of hoping someone would ask me for one, but no one did.

When the last class was over, everyone was cheering and making plans with each other for the summer. And everyone was clearing out their lockers by throwing their old papers and notes and books on the hallway floor. When I got to my locker, I saw this skinny kid who had the locker next to me all year. I had never really talked to him before.

I cleared my throat and said, "Hey. My name is Charlie."

All he said was, "I know."

Then, he closed his locker door and walked away.

So, I just opened my locker, put all my old papers and things in my backpack, and walked over the debris of books and papers and notes in the hallway to the parking lot outside. Then, I got on the bus. Then, I wrote this letter to you.

I'm actually really glad that the school year is over. I want to spend a lot of time with everyone before they leave. Especially Sam.

By the way, I ended up getting straight A's this whole year. My mother was very proud and put my report card on the refrigerator.

Love always,
Charlie

June 22, 1992

Dear friend,

The night before Sam was going to leave made the whole week a blur. Sam was frantic because not only did she need to spend time with us, but she had to get ready to go. Buying things. Packing things. Things like that.

Every night, we would all get together after Sam had just said good-bye to some uncle or had another lunch with her mom or had done more shopping for school things. She was scared, and it wasn't until she had a sip of whatever we were drinking or a hit off of whatever we were smoking that she would calm down and be the same Sam.

The one thing that really helped Sam through her week was her lunch with Craig. She said she wanted to see him to have some kind of "closure," and I guess she was lucky enough to get it because Craig was nice enough to tell her that she was right to break up with him. And that she was a special person. And that he was sorry and wished her well. It's strange the times people choose to be generous.

The best part was that Sam said she didn't ask him about the girls he might be dating even though she wanted to know. She wasn't bitter. She was sad, though. But it was a hopeful kind of sad. The kind of sad that just takes time.

On the night before she left, we were all there at Sam and Patrick's house. Bob, Alice, Mary Elizabeth (without Peter), and I. We just sat on the rug in the "games" room, remembering things.

Remember the show where Patrick did this ... or remember when Bob did this ... or Charlie ... or Mary Elizabeth ... or Alice ... or Sam ...

The inside jokes weren't jokes anymore. They had become stories. Nobody brought up the bad names or the bad times. And nobody felt sad as long as we could postpone tomorrow with more nostalgia.

After a while, Mary Elizabeth and Bob and Alice left, saying they would be back in the morning to see Sam off. So, it was just me,

▷ **19** *Ho-Ho:* small chocolate cake **30** *debris* [də'bri:; BE 'debri:]: untidy mess **36** *put sth. on the refrigerator:* fix sth. on the refrigerator door with a magnet **42** *blur* (n): sth. that cannot be focused on clearly • *frantic:* nervous and hectic **68** *postpone sth.:* put sth. off until a later time

Patrick, and Sam. Just sitting there. Not saying much. Until we started our own remember when.

Remember when Charlie first came to us at the football game ... and remember when Charlie let the air out of Dave's tires at the homecoming dance ... and remember the poem ... and the mix tape ... and Punk Rocky in color ... and remember when we all felt infinite ...

After I said that, we all got quiet and sad. In the silence, I remembered this one time that I never told anybody about. The time we were walking. Just the three of us. And I was in the middle. I don't remember where we were walking to or where we were walking from. I don't even remember the season. I just remember walking between them and feeling for the first time that I belonged somewhere.

Finally, Patrick stood up.

"I'm tired, guys. Good night."

Then, he messed up our hair and went up to his room. Sam turned to me.

"Charlie, I have to pack up some things. Would you stay with me for a while?"

I nodded, and we went upstairs.

As we entered her room, I noticed how different it looked from the night Sam kissed me. The pictures were down, and the dressers were empty, and everything was in a big pile on the bed. I said to myself that I would not cry no matter what because I didn't want to make Sam feel any more panicked than she already was.

So, I just watched her pack, and I tried to notice as many details as I possibly could. Her long hair and her thin wrists and her green eyes. I wanted to remember everything. Especially the sound of her voice.

Sam talked about a lot of things, trying to keep herself distracted. She talked about what a long drive they had tomorrow and how her parents had rented a van. She wondered what her classes would be like and what her eventual "major" would be. She said she didn't want to join a sorority but was looking forward to the football games. She was just getting more and more sad. Finally, she turned around.

"Why didn't you ask me out when the whole Craig thing happened?"

I just sat there. I didn't know what to say. She said it soft.

"Charlie ... after that thing with Mary Elizabeth at the party and us dancing at the club and everything ... "

I didn't know what to say. Honestly, I was lost.

"Okay, Charlie ... I'll make this easy. When that whole thing with Craig happened, what did you think?" She really wanted to know.

I said, "Well, I thought a lot of things. But mostly, I thought that your being sad was much more important to me than Craig not being your boyfriend anymore. And if it meant that I would never get to think of you that way, as long as you were happy, it was okay. That's when I realized that I really loved you."

She sat down on the floor with me. She spoke quiet.

"Charlie, don't you get it? I can't feel that. It's sweet and everything, but it's like you're not even there sometimes. It's great that you can listen and be a shoulder to someone, but what about when someone doesn't need a shoulder. What if they need the arms or something like that? You can't just sit there and put everybody's lives ahead of yours and think that counts as love. You just can't. You have to do things."

"Like what?" I asked. My mouth was dry.

"I don't know. Like take their hands when the slow song comes up for a change. Or be the one who asks someone for a date. Or tell people what you need. Or what you want. Like on the dance floor, did you want to kiss me?"

"Yeah," I said.

"Then, why didn't you?" she asked real serious.

"Because I didn't think you wanted me to."

"Why did you think that?"

"Because of what you said."

"What I said nine months ago? When I told you not to think of me that way?"

I nodded.

"Charlie, I also told you not to tell Mary Elizabeth she was pretty. And to ask her a lot of questions and not interrupt her. Now she's with a guy who does the exact opposite. And it works because that's who Peter really is. He's being himself. And he does things."

"But I didn't like Mary Elizabeth."

"Charlie, you're missing the point. The point is that I don't think you would have acted different even if you did like Mary Elizabeth.

▷ **32** *eventual:* that will happen at the end of a period of time **53–54** *put sth. ahead of sth.else:* act as if sth. is more important than sth. else

It's like you can come to Patrick's rescue and hurt two guys that are trying to hurt him, but what about when Patrick's hurting himself? Like when you guys went to that park? Or when he was kissing you? Did you want him to kiss you?"

I shook my head no.

"So, why did you let him?"

"I was just trying to be a friend," I said.

"But you weren't, Charlie. At those times, you weren't being his friend at all. Because you weren't honest with him."

I sat there very still. I looked at the floor. I didn't say anything. Very uncomfortable.

"Charlie, I told you not to think of me that way nine months ago because of what I'm saying now. Not because of Craig. Not because I didn't think you were great. It's just that I don't want to be somebody's crush. If somebody likes me, I want them to like the real me, not what they think I am. And I don't want them to carry it around inside. I want them to show me, so I can feel it, too. I want them to be able to do whatever they want around me. And if they do something I don't like, I'll tell them."

She was starting to cry a little. But she wasn't sad.

"You know I blamed Craig for not letting me do things? You know how stupid I feel about that now? Maybe he didn't really encourage me to do things, but he didn't prevent me from doing them either. But after a while, I didn't do things because I didn't want him to think different about me. But the thing is, I wasn't being honest. So, why would I care whether or not he loved me when he didn't really even know me?"

I looked up at her. She had stopped crying.

"So, tomorrow, I'm leaving. And I'm not going to let that happen again with anyone else. I'm going to do what I want to do. I'm going to be who I really am. And I'm going to figure out what that is. But right now I'm here with you. And I want to know where you are, what you need, and what you want to do."

She waited patiently for my answer. But after everything she said, I figured that I should just do what I wanted to do. Not think about it. Not say it out loud. And if she didn't like it, then she could just say so. And we could go back to packing.

So, I kissed her. And she kissed me back. And we lay down on the floor and kept kissing. And it was soft. And we made quiet noises.

And kept silent. And still. We went over to the bed and lay down on all the things that weren't put in suitcases. And we touched each other from the waist up over our clothes. And then under our clothes. And then without clothes. And it was so beautiful. She was so beautiful. She took my hand and slid it under her pants. And I touched her. And I just couldn't believe it. It was like everything made sense. Until she moved her hand under my pants, and she touched me.

That's when I stopped her.

"What's wrong?" she asked. "Did that hurt?"

I shook my head. It felt good actually. I didn't know what was wrong.

"I'm sorry. I didn't mean to—"

"No. Don't be sorry," I said.

"But, I feel bad," she said.

"Please don't feel bad. It was very nice," I said. I was starting to get really upset.

"You're not ready?" she asked.

I nodded. But that wasn't it. I didn't know what it was.

"It's okay that you're not ready," she said. She was being really nice to me, but I was just feeling so bad.

"Charlie, do you want to go home?" she asked.

I guess I nodded because she helped me get dressed. And then she put on her shirt. And I wanted to kick myself for being such a baby. Because I loved Sam. And we were together. And I was ruining it. Just ruining it. Just terrible. I felt so terrible.

She took me outside.

"Do you need a ride?" she asked. I had my father's car. I wasn't drunk. She looked really worried.

"No, thanks."

"Charlie, I'm not going to let you drive like this."

"I'm sorry. I'll walk then," I said.

"It's two o'clock in the morning. I'm driving you home."

She went to another room to get the car keys. I just stood in the entry hall. I felt like I wanted to die.

"You're white as a sheet, Charlie. Do you need some water?"

▷ **15** *crush* (n): object of strong, but temporary desire

"No. I don't know." I started to cry really hard.

"Here. Just lie down on the couch," she said.

She laid me down on the couch. She brought out a damp washcloth and put it on my forehead.

"You can sleep here tonight. Okay?"

"Okay."

"Just calm down. Take deep breaths."

I did what she told me. And just before I fell asleep, I said something.

"I can't do that anymore. I'm sorry," I said.

"It's okay, Charlie. Just go to sleep," Sam said.

But I wasn't talking to Sam anymore. I was talking to someone else.

When I fell asleep, I had this dream. My brother and my sister and I were watching television with my Aunt Helen. Everything was in slow motion. The sound was thick. And she was doing what Sam was doing. That's when I woke up. And I didn't know what the hell was going on. Sam and Patrick were standing over me. Patrick asked if I wanted some breakfast. I guess I nodded. We went and ate. Sam still looked worried. Patrick looked normal. We had bacon and eggs with their parents, and everyone made small talk. I don't know why I'm telling you about bacon and eggs. It's not important. It's not important at all. Mary Elizabeth and everyone came over, and while Sam's mom was busy checking everything twice, we all walked to the driveway. Sam and Patrick's parents got in the van. Patrick got in the driver's side of Sam's pickup truck, telling everyone he'd see them in a couple of days. Then, Sam hugged and said good-bye to everyone. Since she was coming back for a few days toward the end of the summer, it was more of a "see ya" than a good-bye.

I was last. Sam walked up and held me for a long time. Finally, she whispered in my ear. She said a lot of wonderful things about how it was okay that I wasn't ready last night and how she would miss me and how she wanted me to take care of myself while she was gone.

"You're my best friend," was all I could say in return.

She smiled and kissed my cheek, and it was like for a moment, the bad part of last night disappeared. But it still felt like a good-bye rather than a "see ya." The thing was, I didn't cry. I didn't know what I felt.

Finally, Sam climbed into her pickup, and Patrick started it up. And a great song was playing. And everyone smiled. Including me. But I wasn't there anymore.

It wasn't until I couldn't see the cars that I came back and things started feeling bad again. But this time, they felt much worse. Mary Elizabeth and everyone were crying now, and they asked me if I wanted to go to the Big Boy or something. I told them no. Thank you. I need to go home.

"Are you okay, Charlie?" Mary Elizabeth asked. I guess I was starting to look bad again because she looked worried.

"I'm fine. I'm just tired," I lied. I got in my dad's car, and drove away. And I could hear all these songs on the radio, but the radio wasn't on. And when I got into the driveway, I think I forgot to turn off the car. I just went to the couch in the family room where the TV is. And I could see the TV shows, but the TV wasn't on.

I don't know what's wrong with me. It's like all I can do is keep writing this gibberish to keep from breaking apart. Sam's gone. And Patrick won't be home for a few days. And I just couldn't talk with Mary Elizabeth or anybody or my brother or anybody in my family. Except maybe my aunt Helen. But she's gone. And even if she were here, I don't think I could talk to her either. Because I'm starting to feel like what I dreamt about her last night was true. And my psychiatrist's questions weren't weird after all.

I don't know what I'm supposed to do now. I know other people have it a lot worse. I do know that, but it's crashing in anyway, and I just can't stop thinking that the little kid eating french fries with his mom in the shopping mall is going to grow up and hit my sister. I'd do anything not to think that. I know I'm thinking too fast again, and it's all in my head like the trance, but it's there, and it won't go away. I just keep seeing him, and he keeps hitting my sister, and he won't stop, and I want him to stop because he doesn't mean it, but he just doesn't listen, and I don't know what to do.

I'm sorry, but I have to stop this letter now.

But first, I want to thank you for being one of those people who listens and understands and doesn't try to sleep with people even though you could have. I really mean it, and I'm sorry I've put you

▷ **55** *gibberish* ['dʒɪbərɪʃ] (infml): meaningless words **63** *crash in* (infml): overwhelm sb.

through this when you don't even know who I am, and we've never met in person, and I can't tell you who I am because I promised to keep all those little secrets. I just don't want you to think that I picked your name out of the phone book. It would kill me if you thought that. So, please believe me when I tell you that I felt terrible after Michael died, and I saw a girl in class, who didn't notice me, and she talked all about you to a friend of hers. And even though I didn't know you, I felt like I did because you sounded like such a good person. The kind of person who wouldn't mind receiving letters from a kid. The kind of person who would understand how they were better than a diary because there is communion and a diary can be found. I just don't want you to worry about me, or think that you've met me, or waste your time anymore. I'm so sorry that I wasted your time because you really do mean a lot to me and I hope you have a very nice life because I really think you deserve it. I really do. I hope you do, too. Okay, then. Goodbye.

Love always,
Charlie

epilogue

August 23, 1992

Dear friend,

I've been in the hospital for the past two months. They just released me yesterday. The doctor told me that my mother and father found me sitting on the couch in the family room. I was completely naked, just watching the television, which wasn't on. I wouldn't speak or snap out of it, they said. My father even slapped me to wake me up, and like I told you, he never hits. But it didn't work. So, they brought me to the hospital where I stayed when I was seven after my aunt Helen died. They told me I didn't speak or acknowledge anyone for a week. Not even Patrick, who I guess visited me during that time. It's scary to think about.

All I remember is putting the letter in the mailbox. The next thing I knew, I was sitting in a doctor's office. And I remembered my aunt Helen. And I started to cry. And the doctor, who turned out to be a very nice woman, started asking me questions. Which I answered.

I don't really want to talk about the questions and the answers. But I kind of figured out that everything I dreamt about my aunt Helen was true. And after a while, I realized that it happened every Saturday when we would watch television.

The first few weeks in the hospital were very hard.

The hardest part was sitting in the doctor's office when the doctor told my mom and dad what had happened. I have never seen my mother cry so much. Or my father look so angry. Because they didn't know it was happening when it was.

But the doctor has helped me work out a lot of things since then. About my aunt Helen. And about my family. And friends. And me. There are a lot of stages to these kinds of things, and she was really great through all of them.

The thing that helped me the most, though, was the time I could have visitors. My family, including my brother and sister, always came for those days until my brother had to go back to school to play football. After that, my family came without my brother, and my brother sent me cards. He even told me on his last card that he read my report on *Walden* and liked it a lot, which made me feel really good. Just like the first time I saw Patrick. The best thing about Patrick is that even when you're in a hospital, he doesn't change. He just cracks jokes to make you feel better instead of asking you questions about feeling worse. He even brought me a letter from Sam, and Sam said that she was coming back at the end of August, and if I got better by then, she and Patrick would drive me through the tunnel. And this time, I could stand in the back of the pickup truck if I wanted to. Things like that helped more than anything.

The days when I received mail were good, too. My grandfather sent me a really nice letter. So did my great aunt. So did my grandma and Great Uncle Phil. My Aunt Rebecca even sent me flowers with a card that was signed by all my Ohio cousins. It was nice to know that they were thinking about me just like it was nice the time Patrick brought Mary Elizabeth and Alice and Bob and everyone for a visit. Including Peter and Craig. I guess they're friends again. And I was glad they were. Just like I was glad that Mary Elizabeth did most of the talking. Because it made things feel more normal. Mary Elizabeth even stayed a little later than the others. I was so happy to have a chance to talk with her alone before she left for Berkeley. Just like I was happy for Bill and his girlfriend when they came to see me two weeks ago. They're getting married this November, and they want me to go to their wedding. It's nice to have things to look forward to.

The time it started to feel like everything was going to be all right was the time when my sister and brother stayed after my parents had left. This was some time in July. They asked me a lot of questions about Aunt Helen because I guess nothing had ever happened to them. And my brother looked really sad. And my sister looked really mad. It was at that time that things started to get clearer because there was nobody to hate anymore after that.

What I mean is that I looked at my brother and sister, and I thought that maybe someday they would be an aunt and uncle, just like I would be an uncle. Just like my mother and Aunt Helen were sisters.

And we could all sit around and wonder and feel bad about each other and blame a lot of people for what they did or didn't do or what they didn't know. I don't know. I guess there could always be someone to blame. Maybe if my grandfather didn't hit her, my mom wouldn't be so quiet. And maybe she wouldn't have married my dad because he doesn't hit. And maybe I would never have been born. But I'm very glad to have been born, so I don't know what to say about it

▷ **7** *snap out of it* (infml): come (back) to your senses **10** *acknowledge sb./sth.* [ək'nɑːlɪdʒ]: show that you are aware of sb. or sth.

all especially since my mom seems happy with her life, and I don't know what else there is to want.

It's like if I blamed my aunt Helen, I would have to blame her dad for hitting her and the friend of the family that fooled around with her when she was little. And the person that fooled around with him. And God for not stopping all this and things that are much worse. And I did do that for a while, but then I just couldn't anymore. Because it wasn't going anywhere. Because it wasn't the point.

I'm not the way I am because of what I dreamt and remembered about my aunt Helen. That's what I figured out when things got quiet. And I think that's very important to know. It made things feel clear and together. Don't get me wrong. I know what happened was important. And I needed to remember it. But it's like when my doctor told me the story of these two brothers whose dad was a bad alcoholic. One brother grew up to be a successful carpenter who never drank. The other brother ended up being a drinker as bad as his dad was. When they asked the first brother why he didn't drink, he said that after he saw what it did to his father, he could never bring himself to even try it. When they asked the other brother, he said that he guessed he learned how to drink on his father's knee. So, I guess we are who we are for a lot of reasons. And maybe we'll never know most of them. But even if we don't have the power to choose where we come from, we can still choose where we go from there. We can still do things. And we can try to feel okay about them.

I think that if I ever have kids, and they are upset, I won't tell them that people are starving in China or anything like that because it wouldn't change the fact that they were upset. And even if somebody else has it much worse, that doesn't really change the fact that you have what you have. Good and bad. Just like what my sister said when I had been in the hospital for a while. She said that she was really worried about going to college, and considering what I was going through, she felt really dumb about it. But I don't know why she would feel dumb. I'd be worried, too. And really, I don't think I have it any better or worse than she does. I don't know. It's just different. Maybe it's good to put things in perspective, but sometimes, I think that the only perspective is to really be there. Like Sam said. Because it's okay to feel things. And be who you are about them.

When I got released yesterday, my mom drove me home. It was in the afternoon, and she asked me if I was hungry. And I said yes. Then, she asked me what I wanted, and I told her I wanted to go to McDonald's like we did when I was little and got sick and stayed home from school. So, we went there. And it was so nice to be with my mom and eat french fries. And later that night to be with my family at dinnertime and have things just be like they always were. That was the amazing part. Things just keep going. We didn't talk about anything heavy or light. We were just there together. And that was enough.

So, today my father went to work. And my mother took my sister and me out to take care of last-minute things for my sister since she's leaving for college in a few days. When we got back, I called Patrick's house because he said that Sam should be home by then. Sam answered the phone. And it was so nice to hear her voice.

Later, they came by in Sam's pickup truck. And we went to the Big Boy just like we always did. Sam told us about her life at school, which sounded very exciting. And I told her about my life in the hospital, which didn't. And Patrick made jokes to keep everyone honest. After we left, we got in Sam's pickup truck, and just like Sam promised, we drove to the tunnel.

About half a mile from the tunnel, Sam stopped the car, and I climbed in back. Patrick played the radio really loud so I could hear it, and as we were approaching the tunnel, I listened to the music and thought about all the things that people have said to me over the past year. I thought about Bill telling me I was special. And my sister saying she loved me. And my mom, too. And even my dad and brother when I was in the hospital. I thought about Patrick calling me his friend. And I thought about Sam telling me to do things. To really be there. And I just thought how great it was to have friends and a family.

As we went into the tunnel, I didn't hold up my arms like I was flying. I just let the wind rush over my face. And I started crying and smiling at the same time. Because I couldn't help feeling just how much I loved my aunt Helen for buying me two presents. And how much I wanted the present I bought my mom for my birthday to be really special. And how much I wanted my sister and brother and Sam and Patrick and everyone else to be happy.

But mostly, I was crying because I was suddenly very aware of the fact that it was me standing up in that tunnel with the wind over my face. Not caring if I saw downtown. Not even thinking about it.

Because I was standing in the tunnel. And I was really there. And that was enough to make me feel infinite.

Tomorrow, I start my sophomore year of high school. And believe it or not, I'm really not that afraid of going. I'm not sure if I will have the time to write any more letters because I might be too busy trying to "participate."

So, if this does end up being my last letter, please believe that things are good with me, and even when they're not, they will be soon enough.

And I will believe the same about you.

Love always,
Charlie

VOCABULARY: "GOING TO SCHOOL IN AMERICA"

Many of the words in this list are American English words which are not used in the same sense in Britain. The term "school" applies to any institution that provides instruction, including universities and colleges (in order to simplify the explanations below, "school" will be used for secondary education and "college" for higher education). The term "student" applies to any person attending any kind of school.

academic scholarship: money provided by an organization (e.g. a college or institution) to help pay for the college fees of students who are academically successful.
bachelor's degree: degree given by a college to a student who has successfully completed a four-year undergraduate study course.
class reunion: meeting of former class members of a high school some time after graduation.
community college: a two-year college which emphasizes training for a career rather than academic education. Community colleges usually serve a certain community and are often supported by it and will take anyone who has graduated from high school.
C: cf. "grades" below.
detention: punishment in which a student is made to stay in school after classes have finished and do special work.
dorm(itory): building on a college campus providing accommodation for many students.
final: one of a series of examinations a student has to sit at the end of an academic year in high school.
fraternity: society of male students at an American college who live together in a fraternity house; selection to the fraternity is by other fraternity members; fraternity societies usually have Greek letters as names (e.g. Alpha Sigma Phi); (cf. also "sorority", below)
freshman: student in the first year of college, or 9th grade in a high school.
grade: 1) letter that stands for a student's achievement – A (excellent), B (very good), C (average), D (poor), F (fail); "straight A's" means that a student has only got grade A's in all his or her subjects.
2) class or year.

graduation: ceremony which marks the departure of students from a school or college after successfully completing the course and receiving a degree or diploma.

graduation cap: special flat hat worn by graduates during the graduation ceremony.

graduate ['grædʒueɪt] (v): leave a school or college after completing the course and receiving a degree or diploma.

graduate ['grædʒuət] (n): person who has completed a course at a school or college and has received a degree or diploma.

graduate school ['grædʒuət]: college which teaches courses for students who have graduated from college with a bachelor's degree.

guidance counselor: person who advises students about their school career.

haze sb.: initiate sb. (esp. a fellow student) into a college or society by forcing him or her to do ridiculous, humiliating or painful things.

homecoming: a yearly celebration in schools and colleges attended by former students.

honors class: an advanced course of study in place of or in addition to the regular course.

junior: student in their next-to-last year of college or high school (= 11th grade).

liberal arts college: college which only teaches the liberal arts (e.g. literature, art, philosophy, history).

locker: small cupboard usu. in a high-school corridor in which a student keeps his or her books and personal things.

major: the subject a college student specializes and receives a degree in (verb: "major in English/Medicine").

middle school: type of school between elementary and high school.

military school: boarding school run by the army which lays particular emphasis on discipline.

open house: a special day at a school or college on which parents and potential students are shown around the school to see what the school or college is like.

permanent record: record of a student's academic progress and behaviour kept by a school.

prom: dance of a particular class at school, usu. held at the end of the academic year.

quiz: short test.

report card: Zeugnis.

SAT scores: the results of the SAT (Scholastic Aptitude Test), which are used to decide which students go to which colleges; SAT scores range from 200 to 800 points in each of the "verbal" and "math" areas of the SAT, and a student can achieve a maximum score of 1600 points.

senior: student in the final year at school or college.

shop class: class in which you learn how to make things with your hands

sophomore: student in the second year of a college or 10th grade in a high school.

sorority: society of female students at an American college who live together in a sorority house; selection to the sorority is by other sorority members; sorority societies are the equivalent for women of fraternities (cf. above).

suspend sb.: forbid sb. (esp. a student) to come to school for a certain amount of time.

undergraduate work: studies done at a college before receiving a bachelor's degree.

valedictorian: the student (usu. the student with the best grades in a year) who makes the "farewell speech" during the graduation ceremony.

yearbook: book that is produced by the graduating class in a school or college containing photographs of students and details of school activities.

Stephen Chbosky was born in 1970. He grew up in Pittsburgh, Pennsylvania, and studied to be a screenwriter at the University of Southern California. He wrote and directed the film *The Four Corners of Nowhere* (1995). Chbosky lives in New York City, and to date *The Perks of Being a Wallflower* is his only novel.